Mar. 13, 1993

For Marty –

Here's hoping these pages & patterns add enjoyment to your sport.

Doan Lurcke

EMERGERS

BOOKS BY

Doug Swisher and Carl Richards

———————————————

SELECTIVE TROUT

FLY-FISHING STRATEGY

STONEFLIES (with Fred Arbona)

EMERGERS

EMERGERS

Doug Swisher and Carl Richards

ILLUSTRATED BY

Mike Gouse

LYONS & BURFORD, PUBLISHERS

Printed in the United States of America

10   9   8   7   6   5   4   3

Library of Congress Cataloging-in-Publication Data

Swisher, Doug.
    Emergers / Doug Swisher and Carl
Richards ; illustrated by Mike Gouse.
        p.   cm.
    Includes bibliographical references and
index.
    ISBN 1-55821-095-4 : $22.95
    1. Aquatic insects—Life cycles. 2. Insects—
Metamorphosis. 3. Fly fishing. I. Richards,
Carl, 1933- . II. Title.
    QL495.5.S93 1991
    595.7092—dc20   90-21032
                                                   CIP

Table of Contents

5

Patterns

45

6

Techniques for Fishing below the Surface

87

7

Techniques for Fishing at the Surface

97

Coda

113

Bibliography

116

Index

118

Acknowledgments

WE have received much welcome help from a number of people and wish to express our appreciation and thanks to the following:

First to Alecia Richards for editorial help, typing, and sacrifice during the research and writing of this book.

To Jack Kiel and Dr. Fred Oswalt for the ingenious construction of the photographing aquarium.

To Nick Lyons for the encouragement to write the book.

Professional entomologists were very helpful in answering questions and imparting information. Professors who helped us: Dr. W. Patrick McCafferty, who was especially accomodating, sending us numerous articles and papers, comparing observations on emergence, and answering our questions; Dr. Rich Merritt, Dr. Ollie Flint, Dr. G. B. Wiggins, who shared information on caddis emergence; Dr. Charles Watson, who gave us valuable data on methods of emergence of *Chironomids;* Dr. Peter Adler, who showed us the bubble ascension of black flies, and Dr. Jerry Nagel for information on fish diet.

Our thanks too to John Young, Brian Osgood, John Krause, Dr. Robert Marcereau, personal fly-fishing friends who helped us collect trout-stream insects (especially caddis pupae—which is lots of hard work!).

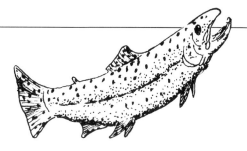

Introduction

THIS study started a long time ago as a simple quest for the secret of the caddis emergence; but it became much more than that. On the following pages we believe the reader will find more information than has ever been popularly available to fly fishermen about the actual methods and mechanisms that caddis pupae, mayfly nymphs, and other aquatic insects employ to propel themselves from the bottom of the stream to the surface, and what happens at or near the surface when they emerge successfully, or die and drown in the attempt.

In many cases the ascension and emergence was not at all as we had believed. The divergence from the so-called norm led to a birth of fly patterns that we felt more realistically imitated the appearance and actions of the naturals during the critical period when the immatures are most vulnerable to predation by trout.

We had always been less than thrilled with our lack of success with existing caddis pupa patterns. We suspected there was something occurring during a caddis hatch that was eluding us, and since very few people have ever seen a live caddis pupa and fewer still a pupa swimming to the surface, we decided the only way to solve the mystery would be to collect many naturals just before a known flush-emergence and watch how they actually got from the bottom to the top.

We began the study by arranging three small aerated aquariums on the bank of the river just prior to the hatch. We then seined the riffles and pools, collecting every type of aquatic insect we could and placed the specimens in the aquariums. Naturally, we captured many mayfly and stonefly nymphs, free-living caddis worms, and a myriad of other aquatic insects; but we found few caddis pupa in the seines. We learned a lot that we didn't suspect about mayflies and other aquatic-insect behavior (which, theoretically, should not have been occurring) but not very much about caddis. Obviously, a different method was needed to collect the mature pupa.

We also noticed that the insects were emerging from our streamside aquariums at the same time of day they were coming off the river, and naturally the fish were rising in great numbers. It was extremely difficult not to give in to temptation and just go fishing, but somehow we managed to overcome our Pavlovian conditioning, at least some of the time.

Because the caddis pupae were safely enclosed in their cases, cemented to rocks and logs, or firmly fixed to the bottom of the river, they could not be gathered easily by seining. So we devised a different and more efficient method of collecting mature pupa, and soon we were watching them ascend in our tanks to the surface film.

Since we were also observing, inadvertently, all different orders of aquatic invertebrates and making new discoveries of many types, the study was enlarged to include some of the other orders. A considerable amount of new information could be, and was, put to immediate practical use. Some of the information required patterns that would act differently in the water from the standard patterns, and it required many hours at the vise to create flies that could be fished to mimic the action of the naturals.

We felt photographic proof of our discoveries was essential—since we had often been disappointed in the past by others who had reported findings that eventually proved false. We wanted and needed to verify our observations, especially the mode by which the various insects ascended to the surface and emerged from the surface to the air; macrophotography seemed best suited to this purpose. However, the focal length in close-up photography is very critical, especially at one-to-one magnification. More extreme magnification compounds the problem. To keep in reasonable focus on a small insect that is swimming, often rapidly, is very difficult at best. If the swimming insect moves laterally just a few millimeters, it is out of focus and this creates a real problem for the photographer.

After considerable experimentation, both with the collections of insects and the photography of their actions, we feel we now have the shots needed to justify the information and new patterns in this book.

We think *Emergers* makes an important contribution to fly-fishing knowledge; we hope readers will think so, too.

Equipment Used for Collecting, Observing, Rearing, and Photographing Aquatic Insects

MUCH of the equipment used in our study for this book was similar to that used in researching *Selective Trout*. We were able to acquire most of the tools inexpensively or construct them easily at home. The study this time, however, mainly involved swimming insects and required some equipment that was a little more elaborate than what we had used previously.

We were interested in discovering exactly how aquatic nymphs and pupae swim from the bottom of the stream to the top, and then their behavior when they arrive at the surface. It is one thing to observe and photograph a subject that is still or immobile, but quite another to photograph an insect that is moving, sometimes very rapidly, in a fluid medium. When

5

using 35mm macrophotography, the focal length between the camera lens and the subject is very critical. If an insect moves laterally, even slightly, it is out of focus. It takes many attempts and not a little luck to get one or two acceptable photographs.

We collected the aquatic insects by three different methods. First, we used a simple hand screen. This we secured to the bottom of the stream; then we dislodged gravel upstream from the net. The current swept whatever floated down into the net, where it was trapped. The specimens were then transferred to a large container or picnic cooler, which we kept streamside. This type of seine must be emptied frequently because the insects can easily escape or be carried away by the current.

We devised what we consider a more efficient seine than the hand screen. We call it a "dip net." It was constructed from a long-handled landing net, with the original coarse netting removed and replaced with fine nylon mesh. This net was long and deep so the captured nymphs were unable to escape. It also allowed us to cover larger areas of stream bottom without the necessity to empty the contents frequently.

The hand screen and the dip net worked well for every type of larvae we needed with the exception of cased caddis pupa. Caddis pupa are firmly attached to logs and rocks on the stream substrate and their cases must be cut or scraped gently from whatever object they are cemented to. Transferring the rocks and logs intact worked best, since even careful removal seemed to damage many cased pupa. Again, we used large coolers to transport the specimens from the stream to the aquarium. We kept them cool with ice—and most insects arrived well and healthy, even on cross-country trips.

Our main rearing tank was a seventy-gallon, six-foot-long aquarium fitted with an under-the-gravel filter that cleansed the water. We used air pumps for oxygenation. A large water pump sucked water from the bottom of the tank and returned it just below the surface; this created a three-mile-an-hour current over the top third of the aquarium, which helped to create a streamlike environment.

Two photographic tanks were constructed from optical glass. They were very narrow: one inch in width, one foot high, and two feet long. These also had air pumps and under-the-gravel filters. The narrow width helped to keep swimming insects in focus, although with the critical focal lengths of 35mm cameras,

Hand screen

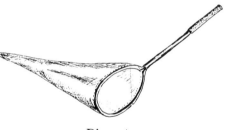

Dip net

Our big aquarium

Our small photographic aquarium, and S.L.R. camera with 2X converters and macrolens it was still extremely difficult to get perfectly focused photos.

We used standard 35mm single-lens reflex camera bodies, each fitted with a 50mm macro lens, for color transparencies and for black-and-white prints. We often attached lifesize adaptors to the camera, and occasionally a bellows or 2X and 3X converters, for more magnification. The macrolens allowed a one-half-to-one magnification. The lifesize adaptors allowed a one-to-one magnification, the bellows allowed up to ten-to-one magnification, and the 2X or 3X converters allowed more distance between the lens and the subject.

We later purchased a super 8mm video camera in order to capture the insects in motion. Our camera was fitted with a telephoto lens and close-up filters. These allowed from one-tenth to one-to-one magnification with the camera remaining a foot or more away from the aquarium. Compared to photographing with a 35mm camera, it is fairly simple to shoot a rapidly moving insect using the video camera. It was aimed at the small aquarium, turned on, and left unattended for an hour or so. If an insect emerged, the camera recorded it. If nothing happened, we merely rewound the tape and tried again. There was no wasted film and no developing fee.

A device is now available in most commercial camera shops that can take a frame from a video tape and make a color print from it. At this writing, these prints are fairly grainy and do not measure up to the quality of a well-focused 35mm print; but this technology is advancing so rapidly that the quality of the prints will surely be much better in a very short period of time.

2

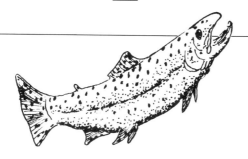

Life Cycles and Methods of Emergence

WITHIN their natural habitat aquatic insects *move!* They move around on the bottom of the stream; they swim from the bottom to midstream; they ascend from the bottom to the top. When they break through the surface tension, they move while shedding their nymphal shucks. If we are to simulate the naturals correctly and fish them effectively, it is not enough to design artificials of the insects as we perceive them when they are immobile or dead. We must know exactly how they swim and their appearance as they swim, as well as their appearance when resting. Unfortunately, all too often our imitations have not been tied in that manner.

This chapter will explain the life cycles of some of the most important trout-stream insects, as well as some of the lesser important orders and what is thought to occur during their ascension to the surface, emergence from the surface, and our own observation of what actually occurs.

MAYFLIES

(Order: Ephemeroptera)

Mayflies exhibit what is known as incomplete metamorphosis; that is, they progress from egg, to nymph, to winged insect without passing through a pupal stage. This is considered to be primitive development. Caddisflies, a more advanced order, are an example of complete metamorphosis. They progress from egg, to larva, to pupa, to winged adult. These differences are very important to the fly fisherman, because the emerging nymphs and pupae look and behave differently.

Mayfly Nymphs *(Hexagenia)* **Swimming to the Surface and Emerging as Adults. Note the Nymph Drifting Just Under the Surface.**

Most anglers believe that when ripe for ascension to the surface, the mature mayfly nymph swims up, somehow breaks the surface film, and emerges from the nymphal case—all of this occurring in a fairly short period of time. It then floats along, for varying lengths of time, on the surface as a dun (subimago), drying its wings. Finally, it flies away to the trees or bushes, where it molts into a spinner (imago).

It is now understood that many species exhibit at least two forms of emergence. Most fishermen believe that a few species such as *Isonychia bicolor* (White-gloved Howdy) swim to the

shore and emerge on land. In this situation, fishermen believe the dun imitation is of no value. Many of the *Isonychia* nymphs will indeed swim to shore before emerging, especially in quiet water, but nymphs of this genus that live in deeper and broader currents often do emerge in the middle of the stream. In this case, the dun imitation is very valuable. Conversely, some species of *Leptophlebia* and *Ameletus* are thought by many fly fishermen to emerge only from water, but this is not so; some individuals crawl partially out of the water and some species completely out. Complete subsurface emergence is found in at least seven genera. None of this behavior is as cut-and-dried as we once thought, and variations from the norm are not only possible but quite common.

The information we gathered proved to us that we did not know as much as we thought about emergences. Many truisms were not true. Mayfly nymphs can and do emerge in almost any manner imaginable. However, the angler is mainly concerned with water emergence and most mayflies are surface emergers. The physical means by which the nymphs get from the bottom of the stream to the top is vital knowledge both for the angler and the fly tyer. Mayfly nymphs crawl, swim, or

Isonychia bicolor nymph in the tail-up position

Mayfly nymphs *(Hexagenia)* **Swimming to Surface**

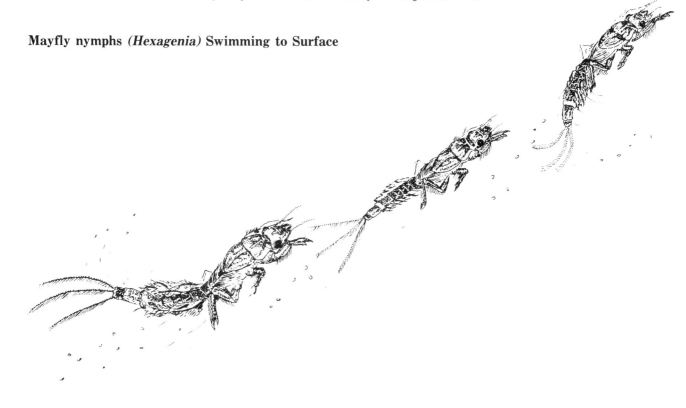

float to reach the surface. The swimming is accomplished by undulating the abdomen up and down in a vertical plane. This movement flips the fringed tails up and down, and both actions provide propulsion in a dolphinlike movement. Mayfly nymphs do not use their legs to swim, although they sometimes "crawl" through the water. The very-fast-swimming mayfly nymphs have interlocking tail fibers that enable them to make rapid sprints. These minnowlike swimmers hold all six legs tucked back under their abdomens. The more clumsy swimmers, such as *Ephemerella*, hold their forelegs forward, out, and down, and the middle and hind legs back, out, and down. In either case, the only time their legs move is when the nymph stops swimming and reaches out to grasp or perch on some object.

The float portion of the swim/float equation is interesting but more complex. Many mayfly nymphs often make several attempts to reach the surface before they succeed. During this time they propel themselves by the up-and-down motion of the abdomen and tails. They swim up toward the surface but then will cease their swimming motion and slowly fall back toward the bottom with abdomen and tails curled up. At this point,

Swimming Mayfly Nymphs

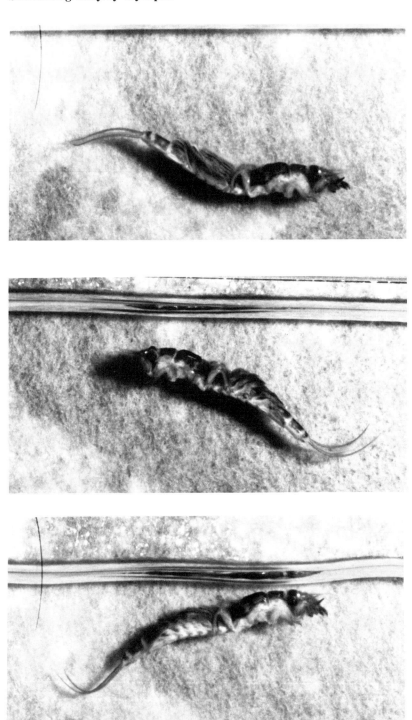

Hexagenia limbata nymphs swimming—with their tails up and down

Ephemerella rotunda nymphs swimming

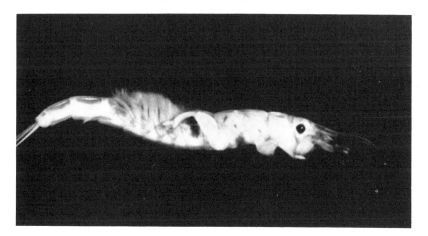

Ephemera simulans nymph in the tail-down position

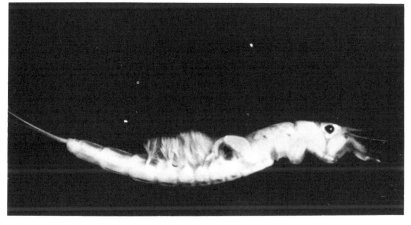

Ephemera simulans nymph in the tail-up position

Isonychia bicolor swimming with its legs tucked back

Ephemerella rotunda swimming with its tail up and legs out in the perch position

Ephemerella invaria nymph— tail up, legs out

they have negative buoyancy and may make many attempts to swim to the surface before succeeding. At some point they achieve a neutral or possibly a slight positive buoyancy. Now when they cease the swimming motion after one of their tries to break the surface, they do not sink, but hover just under the surface. In this position a very narrow white slit is visible on the dorsal of the mid-thorax and often minute air bubbles can be seen escaping from this slit. A very thin layer of oxygen or gas is produced by the insect's cutaneous respiratory system between the inner side of the nymph's cuticle and the outer layer of the dun's (subimago's) body. We believe this process produces the buoyancy. The mayfly nymph is now in a perfect position to break the surface film and sometimes does so rather quickly. After breaking through, it wiggles out of its nymphal shuck and floats on the surface with its legs and often part of its abdomen touching the water. It then dries its wings and eventually flies to the bank of the river. Mayfly duns often float a considerable distance before flying off the surface film.

During the hatch, many individual insects do not get through the film quickly. Some of the nymphs will hover one or two millimeters under the surface for long periods of time. The extent of this long subsurface drifting is surprisingly high. In our observations, it happened about fifty percent of the time. It appears that the nymphs become physically exhausted by their ascension efforts and stop to float for a while to regain strength. They lie very still, without even their gills working much of the time, giving the appearance of death. After a period of time, they will work their gills and legs rapidly and make one or more attempts to break through the surface tension.

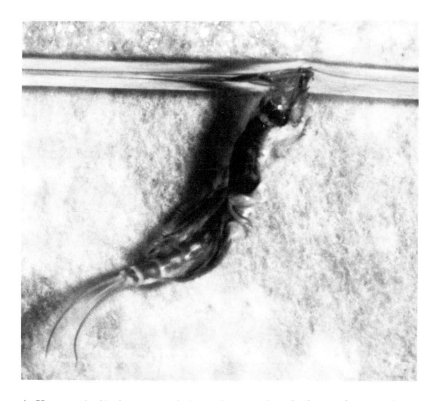

A *Hexagenia limbata* nymph just about to break the surface tension.

The duration of this hovering-recuperation period can be unbelievably long. We have seen it go on for from *five to fifteen minutes*. We found this hard to believe at first; we reasoned the nymph would be swept a mile or more downstream before it could get off the water. This phenomenon was not rare, but common.

Once the nymph does break the surface film (with the dorsal of its thorax) the subimago emerges through the slit in the thorax. The dun's back comes out first, then the lower part of the wings, head, and forelegs emerge. The insect then wiggles and shimmies its abdomen and tails free of the shuck. Its legs and part of its abdomen make contact with the water's surface, which supports the freshly emerged dun. If the wings and/or tails become wetted and entrapped in the surface film, or the tails get stuck in the larval cuticle, the subimago has little chance of escaping.

Ephemerella subvaria emerging from its pupal shuck

Ephemerella subvaria shedding its pupal cuticle

The success of the emergence may also depend on wetting agents present on the surface and the quality of the surface tension or lack of it, all of which will be discussed in a later chapter.

The up-and-down motion of the mayfly nymph ascending to the surface and the dead drift just under the surface strongly suggest two patterns of artificials. These must be fished with two entirely different techniques at hatch time and are very effective when practiced correctly. These two patterns and the techniques to use them are covered in Chapters 6 and 7.

In those instances when mayfly nymphs drift just under the film for many minutes, the apparent surface activity is primarily due to trout sipping slightly subsurface nymphs. When conditions are conducive for rapid emergence, trout take the deeper, up-swimming nymphs and later the floating, winged duns. Factors that result in these variations will be detailed in Chapter 3.

CADDISFLIES

(Order: Trichoptera)

Caddisflies undergo a complete metamorphosis and are considered an advanced order of insects. They progress from egg, to larva (caddis worm), to pupa, to adult. They are closely related to aquatic moths (Lepidoptera), which they strongly resemble.

Once the caddis worm is mature, it builds a case or closes off its existing case, and, over a two- to three-week period, transforms into a pupa.

After cutting their way out of the cocoon on the bottom, some pupa will wriggle out of the case, swim rapidly to the surface, and emerge quickly. Some individuals will lay on the stream substrate, legs curled back under their undulating bodies in what we call the "tucked" position. They will lie in this position for various periods of time, which can be as short as a few seconds to as long as ten or more minutes. As with the mayfly, it appears as if the pupa were building strength and oxygen to attempt the swim to the surface. Sooner or later they will extend their legs, swim up a little, and drift back

Various Caddis Pupa Swimming

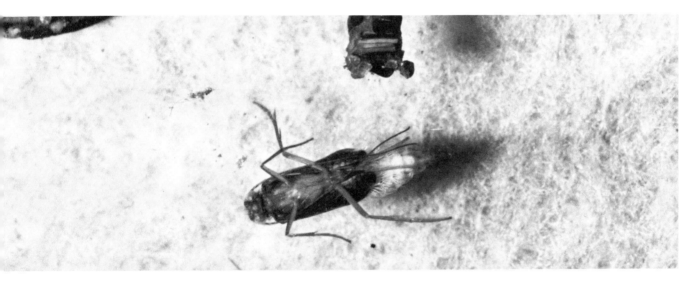

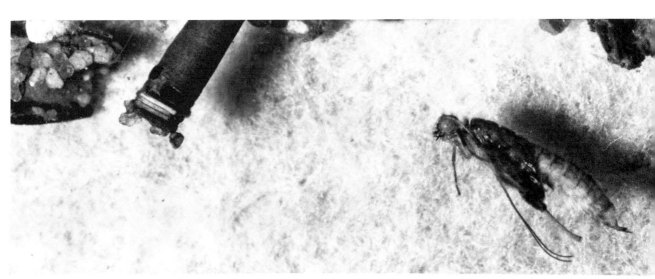

Caddis pupa in the "tucked position"

down, repeating this action several times. Finally, they will dart into the current, swim rapidly to the surface, and emerge.

Many pupa swim on the surface to the shore and emerge on land, and some emerge just under the surface. Species emerging from water break the surface tension and pop out of the pupal shuck much like the mayfly does. There the similarity ends. Caddisflies quickly flip their wings two or three times and, almost immediately, fly off; they do not float for long periods of time as do the Ephemeroptera.

The most important question in our minds was: Exactly how do caddis pupae propel themselves to the surface and how rapidly do they ascend? The answer—for us at least—was at

**Caddisfly Nymphs Swimming
to the Surface**

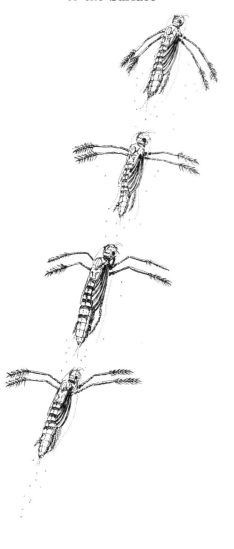

first very elusive; but when we finally discovered what actually happened, it seemed so simple.

We found that *caddis pupae swim in almost exactly the opposite manner of mayfly nymphs.* Rather than resembling the dolphin's form, their legs mimic a breast stroke or the oars of a scull. *They swim almost entirely with their legs.* The middle and forelegs pump back and forth rapidly. The hind legs usually trail back, under the abdomen. This is a striking visual characteristic. While swimming, the body becomes almost perfectly straight and rigid. The long antennae slope back over the top, or can be tucked back under the middle legs along the side of the body.

Caddis pupae do not have tails and therefore need another method of mobility. The middle and forelegs have been adapted for swimming by means of a dense set of swimming hairs on the tarsis. When they are ready, the pupa swim to the surface rather quickly—almost straight up. As with mayflies, some species swim much faster than others.

We will never forget the first time we observed this process from the beginning to a successful emergence. We had carefully cut a number of *Brachycentrus* cases from sunken logs in the river and placed them in the aquarium for photographing. It was mostly luck that we were watching one case that happened to be pointed straight up. Suddenly a black head poked up from the opening in the end of the case. Three quick wiggles of the green-and-black body and the pupa was free from the

One caddis pupa swimming on the surface and one in the tucked position

case. The fore and middle legs extended and the pupa swam rapidly to the surface, where it hit the surface tension and bounced back from the underside of the film. It then relaxed in the "tucked" position and sank down to the bottom where it rested for about five seconds. It then came out of the tucked position and swam quickly, straight up. This time, it successfully penetrated the surface film, emerged, and immediately flew away.

Once the pupae reach the surface, their behavior varies considerably. Quite a few species swim quickly from the middle of the riffle to the shore, resembling a waterboatman skimming the surface of the water. They then crawl out on land to emerge into the adult. Most pupae, however, emerge in the stream, some under water. The adults rise out of the split on the dorsal of the thorax, climb out of the shuck, flap their wings rapidly, and fly to the bank.

Often, however, the pupae appear to become exhausted just beneath the film and to relax, curling up with all six legs

Caddis Pupae Swimming to the Surface and Emerging as Adults

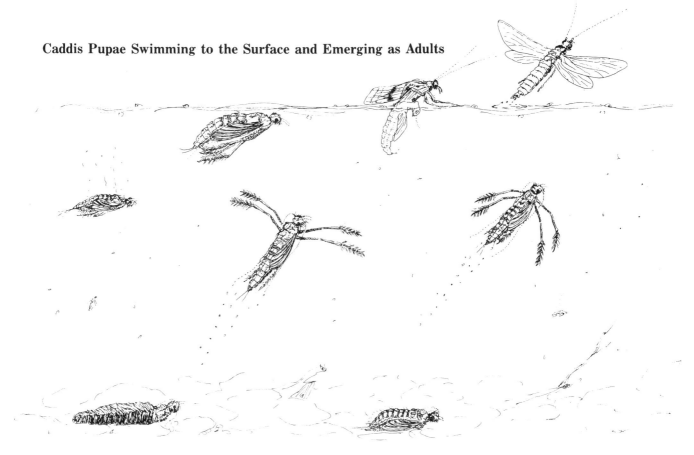

Caddis pupa resting in the tucked position, just under the surface

tucked back under their bodies. They will then undulate their abdomens, which forces water current over their bodies. Spiracles (external openings on the body wall) then take in oxygen through the tracheal system. This replenishes oxygen that was exhausted during the ordeal of the ascent. Many individuals will drift for long periods of time, resting, and will eventually build enough strength for another attempt to penetrate the surface tension.

The middle and forelegs of the pupae seem to do most of the work because they are the ones adapted for swimming, with heavy hairlike fringes. Usually, but not always, the back pair of legs remain tucked down under the abdomen. The long antennae remain swept back over the top of the body or on the sides, tucked under the middle legs, during the ascent.

These different behavioral patterns of caddis pupae prior to emerging into the adult suggest four methods of fishing the hatch, with two different imitations. The most radical is a pattern that would successfully simulate the rapidly pumping legs of the ascending pupa. We will discuss this further and suggest

Extreme close-up of caddis pupa just under the surface

patterns and fishing techniques in Chapters 6 and 7. As you can see, all caddis pupae do not act in exactly the same ways during the hatch. In fact, individuals of the same species exhibit varying emergence patterns. Mayfly nymphs can emerge in a number of ways, and caddisflies, with six times the number of species, give us myriad emergence patterns.

STONEFLIES

(Order: Plecoptera)

Stoneflies exhibit incomplete metamorphosis similar to that of mayflies and are a rather primitive insect. They proceed from egg, to nymph, to adult, skipping the pupal stage. And they do not molt, as the mayfly does, from dun (subimago) to spinner (imago).

The big difference between stoneflies, mayflies, and caddisflies as far as the fly fisher is concerned, is that stoneflies are crawlers, unlike caddis pupae and mayfly nymphs, which swim. Stonefly nymphs possess little swimming ability. When dislodged from the stream substrate, they curl up, legs ready to grab any object they are carried to by the current. They will sometimes move their legs back and forth rapidly, producing some forward motion. Since they are primarily crawlers, they traverse the bottom from the riffles and pools to the stream bank and up to dry land. Here they break the nymphal shuck; a dry imitation is thus of no value *during emergence.*

Some anglers maintain that a few species of Plecoptera do emerge from the stream; in fact, we would have sworn we have fished a little olive stonefly that did just that on the Pere Marquette River in Michigan. However, professional field biologists have told us that "without exception, stonefly nymphs emerge on shore."

Stonefly nymphs

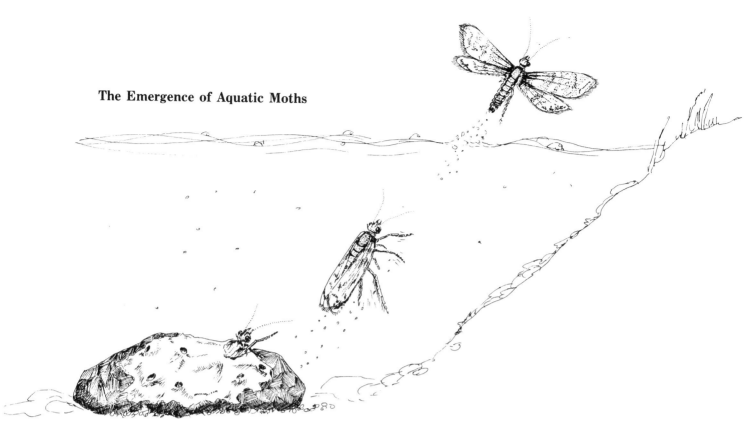

AQUATIC MOTHS

(Order: Lepidoptera)

Aquatic moths exhibit a complete metamorphosis, much like the caddis that they resemble and to which they are closely related. These insects present a very real opportunity for the fly fisherman during the hatch and also during the return egg-laying flight because they are usually present in large numbers. They offer flush emergences that can be extremely rewarding to the knowledgeable fisherman. Few anglers are aware that many species of moths are aquatic. This, and the fact that they are difficult to distinguish from caddisflies certainly leads to a lack of recognition; and the fact that aquatic moths emerge mostly at dusk or just after dark adds to the times when they are commonly mistaken for caddis emergences. As a group, they are slightly larger (#10 to #14) than most caddis species (#14 to #20). The water moth has a long tube that is coiled up under its head when not in use. With a little magnification it can be easily differentiated from Trichoptera, which lack this tube.

The larvae are really aquatic caterpillars, which spin a tough web on rocks or logs on the bottom of the river. These retreats are well camouflaged and difficult to see. In time, the caterpillar turns into a pupa inside its web. Unlike the caddis pupa, which emerges from its case and swims to the surface to emerge as a winged adult, the aquatic moth emerges from the pupa on the bottom of the river as a winged adult. It then swims, rather clumsily, to the surface and flies to the bank of the river. The adult has hydrofuge properties that shed water and its hind legs possess swimming hairs. Trout often engage in feeding frenzies during these flush hatches.

These insects are usually a tan, cream, or buff color and large caddis adult patterns fished wet are very effective when aquatic moths are emerging.

BLACK FLIES

(Order: Diptera)

Black flies, although not usually thought of as trout food, are eaten quite often by trout, especially brook trout, and they also make up a large percentage of the diet of young Atlantic salmon. The black fly population is on the rise in the United States because we are becoming more and more successful in cleaning our trout streams of pollution, resulting in the very pure water the order requires.

Black flies have a complete metamorphosis but the interesting aspect is that they emerge from the pupal case on the bottom and ride to the surface enclosed in a bubble of air that clings to each insect. The bubble is produced between the inner pupal case and the outer adult body by cutaneous respiration.

CRANEFLIES

(Order: Diptera)

Craneflies have a complete metamorphosis. The larvae are huge (one to two inches long). They exist in large populations in many streams. Seasonally, these insects provide one important part of the trout's diet. The larvae or pupae flex their bodies and crawl on the bottom of the stream. They are usually a dirty tan to tannish-brown color, and are sizable enough that large trout will feed on them while ignoring smaller emerging insects. They are sold in some bait shops, where they are called "spikes." They emerge mostly in spring and early summer.

Most pupae crawl out on shore to emerge, so the actual hatch is not of much interest to the angler; but the larval imitations can be very effective.

Cranefly larvae

DAMSELFLIES AND DRAGONFLIES

(Order: Odonata)

Damsel and dragonflies undergo an incomplete metamorphosis. Fish will feed heavily on the nymphs, especially in slow waters near the banks. The nymphs crawl out of the water to emerge, so the dry patterns are not of much importance at this time. The nymphs are quite large and usually good fish will work when they're emerging. A few patterns fished deep, especially in shallow backwaters, will produce some fine trout.

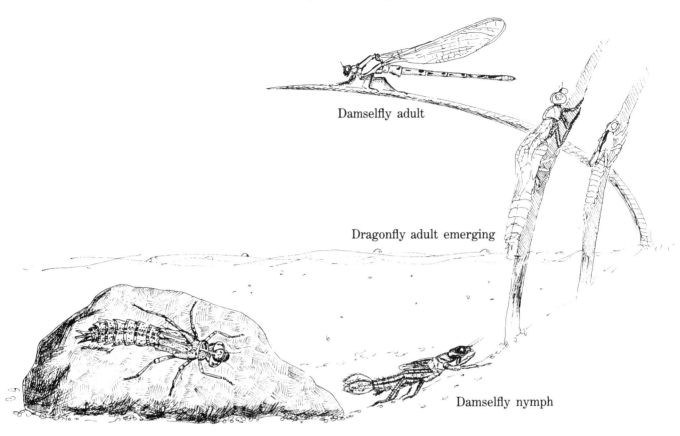

Damselfly adult

Dragonfly adult emerging

Damselfly nymph

Dragonfly nymph

MIDGES

(Order: Diptera; Family: Chironomidae)

Midges exhibit complete metamorphosis. They progress from egg, to larva, to pupa, to winged adult. They vary in size from a fairly large #14 to a tiny #28 and even smaller. The larger species are much more prevalent in lakes and ponds than in streams. The larva of most species live in cylindrical or conical cocoons but some are free-swimming and burrow in the silt or in stone or bark cases, much like caddis pupae. When the pupae mature, they float/swim to the surface by undulating their bodies and terminal swimming paddles (when present). Once at the surface, the pupae drift for a period, split the pupal exoskeleton, and emerge into the adult midge, which flies away rather quickly.

Midge Pupa Swimming to the Surface, Drifting Just Under the Surface, and Finally Emerging as an Adult.

There is disagreement among experts concerning the point of arrival of the pupa at the stream's surface. Some angling authorities state that the pupae drift for a long time before their emergences. Professional field biologists say that the emerging is rapid. Both are probably correct, depending upon water speed and the condition of the surface tension. In streams with a good current, these small insects probably do get off the surface rapidly. In areas with little water movement, they may take more time. Most anglers who fish midge emergences have noticed that at times a floating pupa pattern is effective and at other times the adult dry fly is much better. As with the mayflies, it appears that trout will feed on the stage that lasts the longest. If the pupae hang in the film for a long period, the fish will feed on the pupae. If the adults emerge from the pupal shucks rapidly, they will feed on the winged adult or especially the inbetween stage when the adult is half out of the pupal shuck.

Stream species of midges exhibit the behavioral drift pattern. These flies are especially important to trout fishermen in lakes and slow-moving rivers. This group is widely adapted for almost all ecological niches and is important as a fish food. About two thousand species are known to exist, so many variations of behavior can be expected.

3

Factors Affecting Successful Emergence

THE degree to which given mayfly hatches are or aren't successful has always puzzled us. Some days the insects all emerge successfully and lift off the water quickly. On other days they drift for a long period of time before they take to the air. On many days, half of the insects will become waterlogged, with one or both wings and tails half-drowned in the film. These variations occur not only between species but within the same species. The differences are extremely important to the fly fisherman because imitations should be tied to match the conditions and actions of the insects. After researching these differences, we learned that the factors that affect a successful emergence of aquatic insects include speed of current, lack of current, surface tension, size of the insect, temperature, and wind speed.

CURRENT VELOCITY

Watching the stream closely, we noticed that most aquatic species popped up through the surface film quickly if the stream current was moving at a moderate flow and the surface was agitated or broken by riffles. We began our study by observing the naturals in a small, aerated aquarium. Although the water was moving, it was moving from the bottom to the top instead of across the surface. We were amazed at the very high percentage of insects that did not get through the surface film—and even more so by the numbers that finally *did* get through, but could not acquire flight.

We realized that the conditions we had set up did not effectively simulate a trout stream, so we switched to a six-foot-long seventy-gallon tank equipped with a strong water pump. This created a three-mile-an-hour current across the top third of the aquarium. In this environment, it did seem that many more individual insects emerged successfully—although many still failed. We discovered mayfly nymphs can indeed break the surface film more easily with the help of a current when the surface is slightly riffled. This is especially true of the smaller species. Presumably, the surface agitation lessens the surface tension and thus makes it easier for the small, weaker nymphs to break up through the tension barrier. Larger genera—such as *Hexagenia* and *Ephemera*—have more bulk and seem to have little problem breaking through the barrier, even in still water. We consulted various professional entomologists, who verified our observations.

The information we compiled has a practical application for the fly fisherman. We were able to use the information we'd acquired one September afternoon on the Housatonic River in Connecticut. The Housatonic is a large river with no-kill areas and a good brown trout population. Its long riffles are strewn with rocks and boulders, which form excellent holding water. It also has large, quiet pools with heavy mayfly hatches. That September day, an emergence of tiny Blue-Winged Olives *(Pseudocloeon)* began about 11:00 A.M. Fishing the pocket water in the riffles was productive using #24 Blue-Winged Olive no-hackle dry flies, but as we worked our way down to the huge pool at the end of the fishing-for-fun area, we could not get a rise, even though fish were feeding continuously. Here the fish were taking the nymphs drifting just under the surface. The insects were having trouble emerging and were forced to drift for a long time before breaking through the film. We put on a #22 dark-olive nymph dressed on a wet-fly hook, greased the leader to one inch from the fly, and fished it dead drift in the current. As soon as we switched from a dry fly to a submerged nymph pattern, the browns started to hit regularly. The longer the drifting-nymph stage, the more critical it is to use a submerged fly. Trout will feed selectively on duns or nymphs, whichever stage is longer lasting—and the water type will usually dictate the length of the stage.

SURFACE TENSION

Surface tension, or lack of it, can be vital to the success of an emergence. It is difficult for small mayfly nymphs to penetrate the surface when they have ascended from the bottom of the stream to the top. Once penetrated, however, surface tension tends to hold the insect on the film and helps to prevent it from being wetted and trapped in the film. Certain substances, such as scum on the surface or organic material dissolved in the water, reduce surface tension. Most anglers who cast a fly in a lake in bloom or a lake with dirty water, notice their fly line begin to sink rather quickly, which indicates that it needs frequent cleaning. This will happen because the surface tension is greatly reduced by the scum, which acts as a wetting agent and allows the line to collect dirt.

Surface tension is the tendency of a liquid to behave somewhat like a thin elastic membrane. This is caused by a cohesion of force that causes the molecules of the liquid to be attracted to one another. Thus the surface of water can support a needle or a razor blade when it is placed down gently, even though these objects are much heavier than water.

Mayfly duns have hydrofuge (water repellent) properties. The presence of substances such as scum, dust, or plant pollen on the surface greatly reduces these properties. On very wide rivers, such as the Bow in Alberta, Henry's Fork of the Snake in Idaho, or the Missouri in Montana, the consequences of normal or reduced surface tension can be observed easily. If a crosswind is blowing (and one usually is), the dust, pollen, or scum will be blown to one side of the river. On the windward side, during a really good hatch of duns, literally thousands of insects can be seen with one or both wings and tails caught in the film. On the leeward side, the insects get off the clean surface rather quickly. Trout on the side of the river with the scummy surface will feed mostly on slightly submerged nymphs during the initial stage of the hatch and on crippled duns during the later stage, while fish on the clean-water side will take upwinged dry imitations.

There is probably some interaction between still water, fast water, and scummy water. Possibly the quicker water breaks up the scum while, conversely, the still water allows it to collect. A swift current may reduce the surface tension just enough to allow the smaller insects to break the surface; but it will also sweep away the scum so that when the insect does emerge, there will be no wetting agent present to trap the dun in the film.

TEMPERATURE AND WIND

Factors that affect the speed at which insects—especially mayfly duns—get off the water are temperature and wind velocity. Many anglers have noticed that on sunny, windy days, the duns get off the water fast because their wings dry quickly; but another factor may be even more important. The wing muscles in the thoraxes of insects require a certain minimum temperature in order to work the wings fast enough to achieve flight. Insects can raise this internal temperature, by working their wings, so if the air temperature is slightly below the required flight temperature, the duns can work their wing muscles, warming them just enough to fly. It appears that on cool, cloudy days duns will drift for much longer periods than on warm sunny days, and experience has proven out this surmise.

TIMING THE HATCH

When we wrote *Selective Trout* we talked about our most "pleasant time of day" theory—that an "emergence will occur at the most pleasant time of day for the season of the year." Thus, in early May, the sun warmed the air and water at midday so that the afternoon hours became the most pleasant time of day. Just a few years ago this timetable was very reliable.

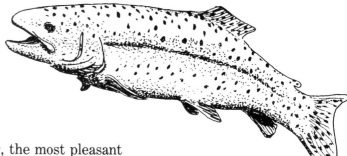

During the month of May of any given year, the most pleasant time of day occurred at or very near 2:00 P.M. (EST) and the Hendrickson hatch regularly began at 2:00 P.M. Ten years ago the Hendrickson hatch rarely started by Opening Day in Michigan (the last Saturday in April). In recent years, however, the climate has become more variable and erratic. Due to unseasonably warm spring weather, the Hendrickson hatch often starts *before* Opening Day. These irregular weather patterns have changed the hatch times and the most pleasant time of day. A couple of years ago, we arrived on the AuSable River on the Friday before the Opener. The weather was very warm. Nighttime temperatures exceeded 70°. In the morning, Hendricksons began showing at 9:00 A.M. and the hatch was over by 10:30 A.M. Most anglers were having breakfast and were not yet out on the stream. The vast majority of them returned from fishing that day and complained that the hatch did not come off. It did. But due to the unseasonable weather, the fish were feeding on Hendricksons while the fishermen were feeding themselves.

It appears that temperature, especially nighttime temperature, is much more important than we thought for all hatches—and even for spinner falls. In the spring, mating flights are supposed to occur at dusk, but it can be very cool at dusk, too cool for flight muscles to function. Much of the time the spinner fall will occur in the morning, just as the sun begins to warm the air, allowing the insects to fly easily.

4

Invertebrate Drift

THE daily occurrence of invertebrate drift brings an added dimension to fly fishing. Many anglers, unaware of the phenomenon, miss it entirely. Invertebrate drift, often called "drift," is a natural event that is well known by biological workers in this field but not recognized by many fly fishermen. It has been found that aquatic insects in the nymph or larval stage drift downstream in a recurring pattern every twenty-four hours. Some drift happens during daylight hours, although most of it occurs in darkness; there are usually two peaks of maximum activity.

Trout-stream insects are usually reclusive; but during the peaks of the drift there is an increase of available food, sometimes an extremely large increase. The larvae are vulnerable to predation during these periods. Drift could be called *an ascension without an emergence*. Examination of the stomach contents of fish prove that they do feed on the drifting insects.

There are three types of drift. The first is a random drift that occurs with lower numbers of insects much of the time. The second is called "catastrophic drift," which is caused by events such as floods. The third is "behavioral drift"—diurnal in nature (recurring in a twenty-four-hour period) and the most important to fishermen. It takes place every day with a high peak occurring just after sunset and a slightly lower peak occurring just before sunrise. These peaks are very light-sensitive and even a full moon will inhibit them. This partly explains why good fly fishing can be had by early-bird fishermen or those willing to stay out after dark. It also explains the old saying, "Trout don't feed well during a full moon." Although a few species exhibit daytime peaks of drift (especially *Baetis*), most prefer darkness. The five major taxa that engage in behavioral drift are mayflies, stoneflies, caddisflies, black flies, and scuds. Absent in drift samples are burrowing mayflies, cased caddis, and midges. We have, however, observed cased caddis swimming, although rather clumsily. It may be that they do drift at times, perhaps in daylight. Some casemakers appear to abandon their cases and drift as worms.

The function of periodic drift has been studied and several theories have been offered to explain this action. The most logical theory is overpopulation of a species, which results in crowding. The nymphs swim up toward the surface and then relax, which allows the current to carry them downstream, thus eliminating the crowding. The magnitude of the drift is considerably higher in riffles. The propensity to drift is generally greater in the later stages of maturation, and greater in warmer months; this coincides with the later stages of most insects.

Another function of the drift may be a search for ideal locations for pupation in caddis worms, or emergence sites in mayflies. Another hypothesis is that the adults fly upstream to ideal spawning sites and then the larvae drift downstream due to overpopulation in these spawning sites and/or to extend the range of the species to the downstream limits of suitable water. This theory cannot hold for crustaceans and some Ephemerids, and there are many exceptions to these general rules, but for our purposes they are not very important.

One benefit of the drift to the fish population may be to relocate mature nymphs or larva from shallow riffles, which are great food factories but rather inaccessible to large trout. The insects drift into the deeper pools where trout can then feed on them more easily. This theory is borne out by studies that show a higher fish population in stream areas with the highest

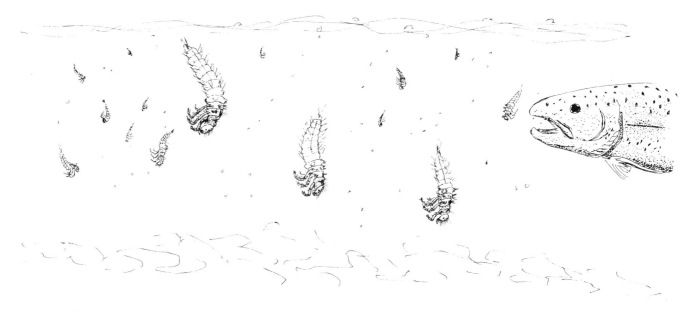

incoming drift. It appears that although fish may feed extensively on the drift, they are at the same time opportunistic, feeding on other available insects that may be present in great numbers—insects not found in the drift.

For practical fishing purposes these factors mean that just before sunrise and just after dark, two drift peaks occur that provide an abundance of food easily acquired, and also opportunistic feeding. Trout will feed heavily but are not particularly selective, and they will strike most good nymph and larval imitations that are presented properly.

During the drift, nymphs and larvae release their holds on the stream substrate and swim up, then relax and allow the current to carry them downstream. This action is repeated a variable number of times. Since trout feed heavily on mayflies, caddis worms, and stoneflies during the drift, suitable imitations fished in the correct swimming manner for each type of insect work well. Stoneflies are crawlers, so they simply let go of the bottom, curl their bodies—sometimes working their legs—and float down in the current. Caddis worms wiggle up a good distance, curl up, and drift down. These two groups should not be ignored because a large number of them are taken during the drift. Mayfly nymphs swim by undulating their abdomen and tails up and down. Imitations tied and fished to simulate this action can be deadly. In streams with

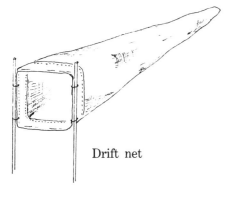

Drift net

larger mayfly nymphs, such as *Stenonema*, good fish will hit these patterns.

Suitable drift imitations for any given time of the year would include a simulation of any species that is about to emerge. Since the more mature forms are the ones that are usually found drifting, they are larger and almost ready to hatch. This makes it easy to choose a correct pattern for fishing the different periods of drift. If you are unfamiliar with the hatches on a stream, simply seine the river and discover which types are in abundance. These will probably be the drifters. If you are scientifically inclined, a simple drift net can be constructed and fastened to the stream bottom just before dark or just before sunrise. It can be examined an hour or so later and it will disclose exactly which species are participating in the drift that day.

This year we witnessed a behaviorial drift of caddis worms. Our big seventy-gallon aquarium (with current) was loaded with rocks from the bottom of the Rogue River, Cedar Creek, and AuSable River in Michigan. This resulted in a very large concentration of caddis worms in a small area. Early in the morning, just before dawn, we switched on the overhead lights on the tank. It was an incredible sight! We saw hundreds of wiggling worms struggling up and drifting down in the flow. The up-and-down wiggling gradually decreased and ended, almost completely, after ten minutes of the aquarium being illuminated. So many worms were struggling in the upper levels of the water that trout faced with such a situation would undoubtedly go into a feeding frenzy.

The phenomenon we observed goes a long way to explain our own fishing experiences. Trout that we have caught early in the morning and late in the evening (on caddis pupa and adults) would often have ten or twenty times the number of worms in their stomachs than other stages of the insect. We wondered how on earth they collected all those worms. The drift that we observed in the aquarium explained this disparity of worms over pupae and winged insects.

Their method of locomotion suggested a new, very deadly caddis-worm imitation. For one thing, it is a fast, almost violent wiggle. Second, the worms swim upside down. The head is down; the abdomen is up. The writhing action seems to sweep the anal process, which usually possesses a brush of hairs or apical bristles, back and forth; this produces an upward movement. A realistic pattern to imitate this action should wiggle easily and be able to be manipulated so that it could be raised straight up and, when pressure is released, sink straight down with its head down. This very effective new tie is detailed in the next chapter.

5

Patterns

WHILE developing patterns to imitate the ascension and emergence of aquatic insects, it is important to keep in mind a number of factors essential for a successful simulation. First, what does the insect look like when it is swimming? Second, what is its appearance when at rest or drifting? Third, can the angler manipulate the artificial in a way that mimics the movements of the natural? These criteria should be rather obvious but there is another surprisingly important and usually ignored requirement: that the artificial be soft and resilient. It must *feel* like the natural to the touch. Most anglers are in agreement that a soft nymph or wet fly is far superior to a hard one.

Even though many patterns have been developed in which every detail of the natural is painstakingly reproduced, these super-realistic ties do not work very well. Most of these patterns are *hard*. Occasionally they may be taken, but they are then spit out so fast the angler does not realize he had a hit; even if he did realize it, he could not strike fast enough to hook the fish. This phenomenon is due to the manner in which trout ingest subsurface naturals. The "take" is definitely not a gulp-and-swallow but rather a bite-down-and-chew method. Once the nymph is in the fish's mouth the trout masticates its food just as a person does. The trout does this not merely once but a number of times—up to nine or ten. If by chance the fish mistakes a twig for a drifting nymph, it is ejected almost instantly. Human reflex is just not rapid enough to respond to this action. The larger the insect, the more chewing takes place—but even #16 naturals are subject to it. We have videotape of fourteen-inch browns taking small *Ephemerella* nymphs, sixteen-inch rainbows taking *Baetis*, and twenty-inch cutthroats taking stonefly nymphs. Every fish masticated the food at least four times and usually twice that number. This easily explains the effectiveness of soft, resilient artificials over the super-realistic hard patterns. The resilient artificial gives the angler much more time to feel or see the take and to set the hook. In fact, we have tried some patterns that feel so like the naturals that trout will actually swallow the imitation and swim off with it.

MAYFLY NYMPH—SWIMMING OR WIGGLE STYLE

Ephemerella subvaria

E. subvaria wiggle nymph

Close-up of thread hinge and of round rubber hinge

The swimming mayfly nymph is tied with an extended body that represents two-thirds of the abdomen. It has some flexible material at the point where it is connected to the hook shank, or with a hinge. The core of the extended abdomen must be as lightweight as possible to accomplish the required action. A 3X fine-wire hook with a ringed eye is ideal. The part of the body that is tied to the main, or front, hook, represents a third of the thorax and the wing case. This must be heavy; if weighted, the lead should be on the bottom and/or sides so that when the fly sinks, it sinks in an upright position. As the fly is twitched up, the light abdomen is pushed down by water pressure. When pressure is relieved, the heavy thorax sinks faster than the light abdomen, so the extended part rises up in a natural position. The flexible joint must be very free-acting, with no tying material in the way to hinder the up-and-down motion.

There are many ways to tie this pattern and many materials can be used. One good formula is to construct the flexible joint first with round rubber or strong tying thread on a fine-wire hook. These make an extremely free-working connection and are easily tied on so that when the abdomen undulates, it wiggles up and down. Furthermore, a fur overbody can be tied over a 3X fine-wire hook with the eye and curve cut off; this is very light.

The front portion, or thorax, can be weighted with lead wire tied on lengthwise, one strand under the hook and one strand on each side; there should be none on top. This ensures that the fly will drift down in the upright position. A heavy wet-fly hook can be used if you prefer not to use weight. Spun fur is wrapped for the thorax and a dark feather section is tied on top for the wing case. Legs are formed with one or two turns of fairly stiff but webby hackle, which is then clipped off top and bottom so only a few fibers extend out and down on the side, preferably three on either side. On all but very rapidly swimming nymphs, some fibers should be forward, two straight out at the side and two sloping back. Remember: *mayfly nymphs do not swim with their legs so this position is natural.* Any webby fibers can be substituted for hackle. The minnowlike nymphs, such as *Isonychia,* hold their legs folded back under the body. When tying a pattern for these genera, six fibers of soft hackle should be laid under the body and tied in. The legs on most mayfly nymphs should be short, about one-third the length of the body.

Tails should be tied on in such a manner as to resemble a horizontal fin. A large bunch of hackle fibers will not appear natural. One of the simplest techniques is to use one tip of a hen hackle, fastened at the end of the extended body in a horizontal position. Three cock-hackle tips can be used if they are fanned out and tied in the same horizontal position; but this is more time-consuming. We do this by first fastening the cock-hackle tips in position with super glue, then wrapping them on with tying thread. This gives a more pleasing look but does not seem to be much more effective than the single hen-hackle tip.

Isonychia bicolor

I. bicolor wiggle nymph

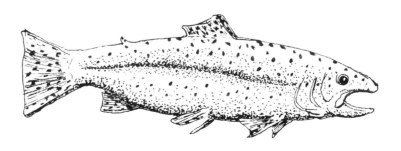

Hexagenia

Hexagenia and *Ephemera* wiggle nymph

Close-up of hinge

Hexagenia and *Ephemera*

Hexagenia limbata (Giant Michigan Mayfly) 18–33mm long
Ephemera simulans (Brown Drake) 10–14mm long
Ephemera guttulata (Green Drake) 18–22mm long

SWIMMING HEXAGENIA

(Overall length does not include tails.)

Hook	Extended part, Orvis #1637 or Tiemco #101, 1X fine-wire, straight-eyed dry-fly hook, #12 for *Hexagenia*, #14 for *Ephemera simulans*. The extended part should not be more than one-third the length of the main hook.
Tails	Three ginger cock-hackle tips tied in on a horizontal plane
Abdomen	Cream spun fur (fine grain)
Gills	A row of small bunches of muskrat underfur tied in along the sides. Small maraboulike feathers found at the base of duck shoulder feathers are even more realistic.
Hinge	Cut off the bend of the hook and loop a piece of strong tying thread through the ringed eye. Tie loop to main hook.
Main hook	Orvis #1642 or Tiemco #3761, 2X heavy, 1X long nymph hook
Abdomen	Continue on main hook with cream spun fur
Gills	Continue on main hook as on extended part
Thorax	Tie cream spun fur with a clump on top to produce dorsal bulge
Legs	Webby but stiff hackle fibers wrapped three or four times and clipped top and bottom
Wing cases	Section of duck primary feathers, very dark
Head	Cream tying thread. You can paint a green eye on the head for more realism.

The genera *Hexagenia* and *Ephemera* have long, strong bodies and are good swimmers. The artificials should be dressed to simulate their shapes.

Ephemerella subvaria (Hendrickson)

This same shape and tie, in various suitable sizes and colors, is used for all the important *Ephemerellas*, including:
E. subvaria (Hendrickson) 9–12mm long,
E. *lata* (Dark Blue-Winged Olive) 6–8mm long
E. *invaria* (Light Hendrickson) 9mm long
E. *inermis* (Pale Morning Dun) 6–8mm long
E. *dorothea* (Pale Evening Dun) 6mm long
E. *grandis* (Western Green Drake) 14–16mm long
E. *flavilinea* (Slate-Wing Olive) 9–10mm long

SWIMMING Hendrickson
(Overall length does not include tails.)

Ephemerella-type wiggle nymph

Hook   Extended part straight-eye fine-wire dry-fly #18, Orvis #1637 or Tiemco #101

Hinge   A small length of strong, flexible tying thread tied in as an underbody and left extending out beyond eye

Tails	Three dark-brown breast-feather fibers, half as long as body and widely spread
Abdomen	Very dark brown, almost black, fine-grain spun fur
Hook for thorax	Orvis #1642 or Tiemco #3761, #16, 2X heavy, 1X long
Hinge	Merely tie in the heavy tying thread that was left extending from eye of the hook that the abdomen or wiggle part was tied on. The eye and head of abdominal hook are cut off with small wire cutters.
Abdomen	Very dark, almost black, spun fur. This should be longer than extended part.
Gills	Pick out fur along sides with dubbing needle.
Wing cases	Black section of duck quill
Legs	Stiff but webby dark-brown cock hackle trimmed top and bottom
Head	Dark brown

Ephemerella nymphs possess robust bodies and are good—but rather clumsy—swimmers when compared to the very fast minnowlike swimmers such as *Isonychia* and *Callibaetis*. The artificials should reflect this in their shapes and be manipulated to imitate the movement of the naturals.

When tying the various species of *Ephemerallas*, you should refer to *Selective Trout* for the colors of each individual species.

Isonychia bicolor (White-Gloved Howdy)

These are the very fast minnowlike nymphs. They have longer, more slender bodies than the robust *Ephemerella*. Other families that have different sizes and shades but the same general shape are:

Baetis 4–10mm long
Paraleptophlebia 7–9mm long
Pseudocloeon 4–5mm long

Siphlonurus 12–15mm long
Callibaetis 8–13mm long
Isonychia 13–16mm long

SWIMMING ISONYCHIA NYMPH
(Overall length does not include tails.)

Hook	Extended part, #18, 1X fine dry-fly, straight-eye, Orvis #1637 or Tiemco #101
Tails	Three wide-spread webby dark bronze blue-dun fibers
Hinge	A piece of round rubber tied in the length of hook and left extended past eye so it can be lashed to main hook
Abdomen	Very dark gray spun fur
Gills	Pick out the fur at sides with dubbing needle to simulate gills
Wing cases	Section of duck primary feathers (black) or a bunch of black marabou fibers tied on top to produce bump
Legs	Webby bronze blue-dun fibers tied in beard style under the body
Head	Brown tying thread

Any one of the three hinge types we have recommended for the previous patterns can be used on any swimming nymph you wish to tie. In fact, many more types are possible. It is important that the extended part swings freely and the connection is strong so it will not be pulled off when playing a fish. All hinge types are good, so it's really what works best for you.

Refer to *Selective Trout* for the colors of individual species.

Epeorus and *Stenonema*

Epeorus pleuralis (Quill Gordon) 9–11mm long
Stenonema fuscum, vicarium, ithaca (March Browns)
10–16mm long
Stenonema canadense (Light Cahill) 8–11mm long

These genera have essentially the same shapes as the robust *Ephemerellas*, except that their tails and legs are longer and the bodies are flattened. A flat body can be dressed by trimming the spun fur on the top and bottom and picking out the sides.

Obviously, many variations on these patterns can be substituted and probably will be. For instance, on larger species, the tip of a toothpick can be used for the underbody of the abdomen. Since the wood will float, the abdomen will undulate up and down as the nymph is worked. Even better, the tip of a Stim-u-dent (available in any drug store) will be much softer than a toothpick and will be masticated by the fish. When dressing these patterns, the proportions should be correct. The wiggle part (the tails and abdomen) must not be longer than the affixed part.

These patterns encompass all the required criteria for a successful simulation of a mayfly nymph ascending to the top for emergence or a natural becoming more active just before emergence. They can also be fished to imitate a natural perfectly during behaviorial drift. The angler is able to work the fly so that it resembles the action of the naturals. The patterns resemble the naturals both when swimming and while drifting down. The artificial is soft and resilient, so the trout will not immediately eject it once it is taken.

The wiggle pattern is not difficult to tie in normal sizes. With very small species (smaller than #16), these ties are not practical and probably not necessary. For the imitation of mayfly nymphs smaller than #16, it is enough to use a very short extension for the abdomen behind the hook so that it can achieve that curled-up look of the natural nymph when at rest or drifting downstream. This extension can have as its base a piece of tying thread with the fur wrapped around it. The tails can be three fibers from some soft feathers such as partridge. This fly will undulate a little—and that is all that is necessary.

Drifting mayfly nymph

Drifting mayfly nymph imitation

DRIFTING NYMPHS

The pattern we use to simulate a mayfly nymph drifting just under the surface is one of the least difficult artificials to tie.

Remember, the larger nymphs have enough strength to break right through the film; it's the smaller insects that have trouble and tend to drift for long distances. These are usually #14 and smaller. These are the genera that trout take just under the surface because they spend so much time there and fish get attuned to seeing them in this position. The natural nymphs float downstream barely submerged, without moving gills or legs or abdomen most of the time. When trout are feeding on these drifting nymphs, a simple fur-bodied artificial with three widely spread short tails, six fanned-out legs, and a dark thorax is an excellent representation of the natural. It is very easy to master the technique of fishing this pattern.

Drifting Mayfly Nymphs

These are exactly the same patterns as the swimming patterns except that they are tied on an Orvis #1638 or Tiemco #5212, 2X long, 1X fine dry-fly hook of the correct length for the natural. They are fished just under or at the surface. They do not, of course, have an extended flexible abdomen. Drifting nymphs are much more important in medium, small, to very small species such as *Baetis*, Ephemerella, and *Pseudocloeon* because these less-robust species have much more trouble breaking the surface tension and tend to drift much longer as nymphs than do the larger species. A piece of closed cell foam can be used for the wingcase to provide flotation.

EMERGING DUN

Sometimes the trout will prefer the stage we call the emerging dun. This is the moment when the natural is pulling out of its nymphal shuck but is still half in, half out. These periods seem to occur when the nymphs have little trouble breaking the film and do not drift for great lengths of time. They usually are hatching from the water with a moderate-to-fast current. This is a most vulnerable period for the naturals because they are on the surface; and since they are not fully out of the nymphal case, they cannot immediately fly away. The fish seem to realize this period of vulnerability and take advantage of it. This

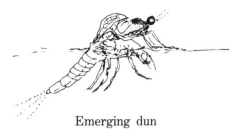

Emerging dun

Emerging dun imitation

phenomenon is related to medium to large flies, #14 to #8, since these species have less trouble breaking the surface tension as nymphs. They sometimes can be effective on very small species, too.

The emerging patterns are tied with an extended body (one half the length of the normal body) of cock-hackle feather—the color of the natural nymph's body or a wisp of fur. The dun's body is of spun fur, two-thirds the length of the normal body length. The wings are a feather section from a duck quill or duck rump tied in a small loop front and back to simulate a period when the wings are bursting out, but not yet fully out. The legs are three short fibers on each side, front to back. They should not be more than two-thirds the length of the body. The easy way to tie these in is to wind a short but webby stiff hackle (or other fiber) once or twice and clip it off, top and bottom.

EMERGING DUN PATTERN

Mayfly emerger (wet)

Hook   Orvis #1638 or Tiemco #5212, 2X long, 1X fine
dry-fly hook

Shuck   Medium bronze blue-dun hackle tip tied in at
bend of hook. This can be tied reverse style for
a more realistic appearance. A wisp of underfur
one-half the length of the body can be
substituted for the hackle tip. This creates a

very realistic, shiny simulation of the trailing shuck. Shucks of mayfly nymphs should be the color of the nymph's body.

Body Spun fur of correct shade for the species to be imitated

Wing Feather section of a duck quill, or hen-hackle fibers, or duck rump tied in a small loop over back, or short and out

Legs Webby but stiff cock hackle wound no more than twice and clipped top and bottom. These should not be more than two-thirds the length of the body.

Mayfly emerger with reversed hackle for cuticle '

This pattern serves a double purpose. It represents not only an insect at a certain vulnerable stage of successful transformation but also simulates a stage of those considerable numbers that do not successfully emerge but become stillborn.

FULLY EMERGED DUN

The best patterns for fully emerged duns, those that have successfully emerged and are floating on the surface drying their wings, are the sidewinder no-hackle and hairwing no-hackle. These patterns were first mentioned in *Selective Trout*. They were then and remain the most effective artificials when trout are feeding selectively on subimagos on the surface. The sidewinder's only drawback is the fragility of its wings, which tend to become split after landing a few fish. If the barb of the hook is bent down, the wings will last much longer, since most of the damage to the wings is really done when you remove the hook from the trout's mouth. Practically no fish are lost when using barbless hooks and considerably less damage is done to the trout. It really does not reduce the fly's effectiveness even when the wings become frayed. Trout don't seem to care if the fly doesn't look pretty. Of course the hairwing no-hackle is very durable.

Mayfly dun (subimago)

SIDEWINDER NO-HACKLE DUN

Hook Orvis #1638 or Tiemco #5212, 2X long, 1X fine dry-fly hook

Tails High-quality cock-hackle fibers widely split, one-half length of body

Body Fine-grain spun fur

Wing Two sections of duck quill feathers tied so the sections come out from the sides of the body. These wings should slope back over the body a little. They should not be perfectly upright.

Sidewinder no-hackle dun

Hairwing No-Hackle

This pattern, which was our original no-hackle (introduced in *Selective Trout*), is a great floater and very durable. It is the same tie as the sidewinder with the exception of the wing, which is tied with some type of hair, usually deer. Select a shade of hair that best matches the wing of the natural you're trying to imitate and fan it from waterline to waterline. With the hair splayed out in this half-circle configuration, the stability and flotation of the fly are greatly increased.

Hairwing no-hackle

V-HACKLE DUN

Another very effective pattern that not only provides an excellent imitation of a freshly hatched dun but also has great durability is the V-hackle dun, also described in *Selective*

Ephemerella inermis nymph

Isonychia bicolor nymph swimming—bottom view showing legs tucked back under body.

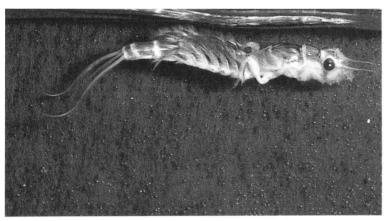

Hexagenia limbata nymph swimming

Ephemerella invaria nymph swimming to the surface

A rare view of a mayfly nymph (*Ephemerella lata* here) half out of its nymphal cuticle

Ephemerella inermis subimago

Mayfly nymph with its tail in the down position

Hexagenia imitation, tail down

Hexagenia imitation with tail in the level position

Isonychia nymph with tail in the up position

Hexagenia nymph with tail in the up position

A Hendrickson wiggle nymph and a Pale Morning Dun emerger

Emerger with wings out of its shuck—shuck is made from a reversed hackle tip

Paradun with hen hackle-tip wings and hackle on the bottom of the hook

Paradrake with elk-hair wing and body

Swimming caddis worm—they swim tail and not *head* up

Swimming caddis worm imitation

Natural caddis pupa swimming

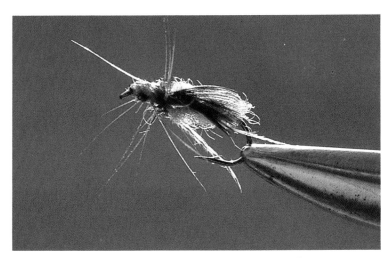

Artificial caddis pupa—to imitate swimming natural

Caddis emerger, with cuticle made of trilobal nylon

Rubber-legged caddis pupa

Trout. This fly has either a single upright wing of such feather fibers as turkey flats, duck side feather, hackle fibers, or hair, or a pair of wings that can be constructed of a wide variety of materials: duck shoulder feathers, breast feathers, hair, hackle tips, or cut wings. Any of these will provide a good silhouette. Short, stiff cock hackle is wrapped behind and in front of the wing and clipped top and bottom. These fibers act as outriggers and keep the fly floating in an upright position. Tails are cock-hackle fibers widely split.

Hook	Orvis #1638 or Tiemco #5212, 2X long, 1X fine dry-fly hook
Tails	Two or three stiff cock-hackle fibers
Body	Fine-grain spun fur
Single wing	Single clump of deer hair or clump of hen-hackle fibers or clump of turkey fibers or any other webby fibers such as duck rump
Divided wing	Duck shoulder feathers, or cut wing from cock hackle, or cut wings from shoulder feathers of other birds
Hackle	Stiff cock hackle wrapped no more than three times and clipped top and bottom

V-hackle dun

PARADUNS AND PARADRAKES

The Paraduns are similar to the V-hackle Duns. The tails, bodies, and wings are the same but the hackle is wrapped hori-

Paradun

Paradrake with hair wing

Paradrake

Paradrake with duck shoulder-feather wing

zontally around the base of the wing, parachute style. The hackle can also be wrapped under the body (around a loop of the hackle stem) for more realism. This technique is more time-consuming but it is worth the effort.

The Paradrakes are the same as the Paraduns except that they have an extended body of elk or deer hair. This is an excellent pattern for the larger drakes, such as the Eastern Green Drake, Brown Drake, Western Green Drake, and Giant Michigan Mayfly. The smaller hooks and hollow extended bodies allow for a much lighter artificial for the overall size. As in all mayfly-dun imitations, the wing should slope back over the body in a flat plane. An upright shaving-brush appearance looks bad and is not natural.

TRICO PARADUN
(Under-Paradun style)

Trico dun, with cream abdomen

Hook	#18–#24, Orvis #1509, Tiemco #100
Thread	8/0, to match body color
Tails	Light gray cock-hackle fibers
Abdomen	Olive to light-gray thread or fur
Body	Dark blackish-gray Belgian mole
Wing	Off-white snowshoe rabbit foot hair
Hackle	Grizzly, parachute

TRAPPED DUNS

Trapped dun

When fish are feeding on duns whose wings have become wetted and are trapped on the surface film, the best pattern is a no-hackle dun with divided quill wings that has been deliberately tied to fall on its side.

One wing will lie on the water while the other wing is above the surface. Instead of tying the fly sidewinder style, merely mount the wings on top of the hook shank. Since there is nothing to keep the fly upright, it will fall over.

Trapped duns are most often found on the windward side of the river, in areas of slow current where the surface tension has been greatly reduced by scum.

Sidewinder tied so that it will
fall over

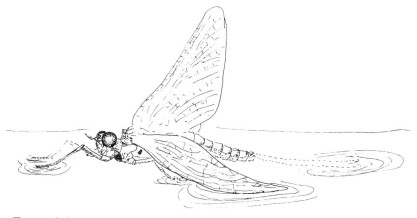

Trapped dun

CADDISFLIES

(Order: Trichoptera)

Caddis Worms

CADDIS worms swim with an unusual violent motion, as explained in Chapter 4. They wiggle their abdomens rapidly back and forth, producing upward movement. Most importantly, *they swim with the head down and the tip of the abdomen up.* This swimming of caddis worms in huge numbers usually takes place early in the morning or late in the evening. However, certain genera, such as the very large *Dicosmoecus* (Giant Orange Sedge) do exhibit drift during late afternoon. The various species of *Dicosmoecus* are extremely important in the western states because they are so large (up to 35mm) that even adult steelhead will feed on them. Their daylight drift should definitely be taken advantage of by anglers seeking big trout.

A pattern to imitate these swimming worms must look like a worm—it must wiggle and it must be tied so that it can be fished ascending and descending, *head down.* We believe the following pattern fulfills all these prerequisites.

SWIMMING CADDIS WORM

Swimming caddis worm

Hook   Extended part, Orvis #1637 or Tiemco #101, 1X fine dry-fly hook, straight eye

Abdomen	Usually dirty olive or dirty tan, fine-grain spun fur
Thorax and legs	Four or five turns of brown marabou clipped on top and sides. The clipped dorsal looks like the thorax. The unclipped ventral represents the legs.
Head	Dark brown, tied in at bend of hook. The bend is then cut off with wire cutters.
Main hook	Orvis #1642 or Tiemco #3761, 2X heavy, 1X long, wet-fly hook, #16–#12 depending on size of worm
Hinge	A loop of strong tying thread is placed through the ringed eye of the extended hook and lashed to the main hook shank.
Remaining abdomen	Fine-grain spun fur, dirty olive or dirty tan
Tail fringes	A wrap of creamy marabou tied in at eye of hook

Swimming caddis worm

Swimming caddis worm imitation

A caddis-worm imitation tied in this manner can be fished head down and will wiggle if manipulated correctly. When the leader

is pulled up, the light hook on the extended body will straighten. When pressure is relaxed, the heavier wet-fly main hook will sink faster than the light look, so the extended part will flex up.

There are all colors of worms but the most common by far are dirty olive, dirty tan, and bright green in the 1½″ to ¾″ overall length range. Some regionally important species such as the late-summer #14 White Miller (this is really a cream-wing, yellow-green-body caddis) in the East and Midwest, and the very large species of fall-hatching genus *Dicosmoecus* #2 to #8 (Giant Orange Sedge) are a few of the exceptions. When they are found, they must be imitated correctly in size, shape, and color, at least to the family level, because they do create tremendous rises. See *Caddisflies* by Gary LaFontaine for sizes and colors of important genera and species.

Caddis Pupa

Caddis pupae swim to the surface using their first two pairs of legs, which give the appearance of being much longer than most mayfly nymphs' legs. The long antennae are held back over the top of the body or under the hind legs and the hind legs are tucked back under the body. When swimming, the fat, short abdomen is ridged and the dark wing cases are positioned to the sides and under the body and are very noticeable. Of course, all these factors must be incorporated in the artificial pupa, but the most difficult is the action of the legs. These pump back and forth very rapidly and are a very visible characteristic. This action must be taken into consideration when designing the artificial.

When the caddis pupa chews its way out of its case on the bottom of the river, some species will swim up a short distance, then drift back to the bottom to rest. They will repeat this action a number of times until they finally swim rapidly to the surface and emerge into the winged adult; some species swim up just after they are free of the case. A number of species, upon reaching the surface, will skate over the water to shore, emerging into the adult on land. Fortunately, all three behaviors may be imitated by the same pattern.

A very effective and easy-to-tie pattern is similar to a soft-hackle fly. We have always believed the success of the soft hackle was due to its resemblance to a caddis pupa. A fat fur body of the appropriate color (usually tan, green, or yellow) is wrapped on the hook. Then a stiff but fairly webby cock hackle or a hen hackle is wrapped in at the head. This hackle should be as long as or a little longer than the body. It is wound on in reverse: that is, the fibers point forward. When tied in this manner, the hackle will be pulled back when the nymph is twitched and released forward when pressure is relieved, thus simulating the back-and-forth motion of the natural's legs. Only two or three turns of the hackle should be used, for we are imitating six legs and two antennae—and dozens of fibers are thus not realistic. The head is then tied off and a black felt pen with indelible ink used to paint on the dark wing cases. This pattern is simple and easy to tie, but meets all the requirements we have listed. When you replace the artificial in your fly box, pull the hackle forward or you may permanently crease it to the rear and negate the action of the legs.

SIMPLE SWIMMING CADDIS PUPA

Caddis pupa—soft-hackle type with legs forward

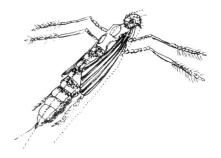

Swimming caddis pupa

Hook #14–#20 for most species, 1XL, 2X heavy, nymph hook, Orvis #1642 or Tiemco #3761

Body Fine-grain spun fur, short and fat, usually olive or tan

Simple swimming caddis pupa

Realistic swimming caddis pupa

Wing cases	Dark brown or black painting on the fur body with a waterproof marking pen
Legs	Two or three turns of webby cock hackle tied in so fibers slant forward. Hen hackle or partridge may also be used.
Head	Dark brown or black

A slightly more difficult pattern, which is somewhat more realistic, would be to tie in the wing cases using feather segments. Two long antennae of soft feather fibers can be laid back over the top of the body or underneath for antennae. Then the stiff but webby hackle, or partridge, should be wound on, reverse-style, at the head. In this case, it is better to trim off the hackle, top and bottom, because we have already simulated the antennae.

REALISTIC SWIMMING CADDIS PUPA

Hook	Orvis #1642 or Tiemco #3761, 2X heavy, 1X long, nymph hook, #14–#20
Body	Fine-grained spun fur, usually olive-tan or bright green
Wing cases	Tips of small feathers found at the base of duck, starling, crow, and similar wings. Black or brown, depending on species
Antennae	Brown speckled feather fibers such as barred wood duck or dyed-brown mallard flank tied under body to slope back past bend of hook
Hackle	Webby cock or hen hackle wrapped and clipped top and bottom, usually black or brown
Head	Brown tying thread

If these two patterns are to be fished drifting slightly under the surface or skittered on the surface, the hook should be an Orvis #1638 or Tiemco #5212, 2X long, 1X fine TD eye dry-fly hook.

Small round rubber effectively represents legs and can be substituted for the first and second pair of legs. This material is nicely resilient and vibrates well in the current or when manipulating the fly.

ROUND RUBBER-LEGGED SWIMMING CADDIS PUPA

Round rubber-legged swimming caddis pupa

Swimming caddis pupa—rubber-leg type

This is the same pattern as the realistic caddis pupa except that the legs are tied in at the sides, so that they slope slightly down and forward. They are usually constructed of .010 round rubber. Smaller and larger diameters are available. The strips can be colored with waterproof marking pens.

Emerging Adult Caddis and Crippled Adult

At the point when the pupa breaks the surface tension, there is a brief period of time when the emerging adult is highly vulnerable. As it is climbing out of its pupal shuck, it cannot yet fly away and trout will take the natural at this point. The pattern is very similar to the emerging mayfly dun. A tip of a light-bronze blue-dun cock hackle should be tied in at the bend of the hook to simulate the pupal shuck that is being extruded—or a wisp of light-tan trilobal nylon. Wrap a short fat body of spun fur and tie in a small bulge of feather fibers on top for the unfolding wings. Then wind two turns only of stiff cock hackle at the head; clip this off top and bottom. These imitate the six legs and the long antennae that, at this point, have become uncased. This pattern, like the mayfly emerger, serves two purposes. It is a good imitation of the adult natural at a vulnerable moment and it also resembles those crippled individuals that become stuck in the case and never do get out. Most caddis shucks are translucent, almost transparent, with a slightly bronze-metallic sheen. This is true for caddis but not mayflies, which have a denser cuticle that is the color of the nymphis body. A good substitute for the bronze hackle is a wisp of light-tan sparkle yarn. This material is both translucent and has a metallic sheen. It produces a very realistic imitation of a pupal shuck.

EMERGING ADULT CADDIS

Caddis emerger with trilobal nylon for pupal shuck

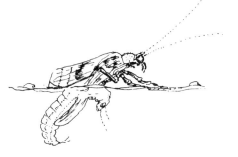

Emerging adult caddis

Emerging adult caddis imitation

Hook	Usually #14–#20, 2XL, 1X fine, TD eye, Orvis #1638, Tiemco #5212
Antennae	Tie in, first at head, two long (usually length of body but for some species much longer) guard hairs from mink tails or any other suitable hair
Pupal shuck	Tip of a shiny light-bronze blue-dun hackle tip, or a piece of light-tan sparkle yarn. The hackle tip can be reversed for more realism.
Body	Short fat spun-fur body (black to green to tan to cream, depending upon species)
Wings	A short loop of feather fibers or a short bunch of deer hair sloping back over body (cream to tan to dark brown) or duck rump
Legs	Short stiff cock hackle wrapped not more than three times and clipped top and bottom

Adult Caddis

The Hen Caddis, first introduced in *Selective Trout*, is sometimes effective for the fully emerged adult. We have had days when it was taken often and other days when it was completely ignored. Those failures probably occur when trout are feeding mainly on ascending pupa. The pattern consists of a fat fur body, and a short cock hackle wound palmer style but very sparse. Then two hen-hackle tips are tied tent-shaped in over the top. A no-hackle deer-hair caddis (Neff Caddis) is sometimes good also.

The Henryville Special, an old standby, is occasionally effective at this time but is more intricate to tie. These three patterns are very good fishtakers when caddisflies are on their return flight and during the egg-laying stage.

The new no-hackle caddis with a wing of duck rump is proving very deadly.

The most common sizes for caddis adults are #14 to #20. A few very important species are much larger and some species are much smaller—but for all but the specialized situation, sizes #14 to #20 are all that you will need.

The most common body colors start in the spring as the darks, black or very dark gray. Then the colors change to olive and tan; in August, some species are cream. As autumn approaches, the colors revert back to olive and tan and then at last to the very dark colors again.

Adult caddisfly

Henryville Special

No-hackle deer-hair caddis

STONEFLIES

(Order: Plecoptera)

Stonefly nymphs are clumsy swimmers at best. Since they crawl along the bottom of the river, then out to the shore before emerging, the imitation must be fished in this manner. During the migration toward shore, the pattern should be fished on the bottom. It must be soft and resilient, ensuring that the trout do not eject it quickly, and the legs should move back and forth.

Hen caddis

Rubber-Leg Stonefly Nymph

Any standard fur-bodied imitation in the correct size and color will work. Replace the usual fiber legs with six round-rubber strands. They should be half the length of the body. These legs will vibrate nicely as you work the pattern slowly—and deep—toward shore.

Stonefly nymph

Rubber-legged stonefly nymph

RUBBER-LEG STONEFLY NYMPH

Rubber-legged stonefly nymph

Hook	#4-#10, 3XL Orvis #1526, Tiemco #5263
Thread	Dark brown, 3/0
Tail	Speckled brown hen
Body	Medium reddish-brown fur
Rib	Dyed brown mono
Legs	.030–.035 diameter round rubber, dyed brown
Wing case	Dark-brown furry foam or dark-brown mottled turkey quill

Drifting Stonefly Nymphs

Occasionally, stonefly nymphs will lose their grip on the stream substrata and be swept downstream with the current. They will then curl up with legs extended, waiting to re-establish a firm position. During this "behavioral drift," the nymphs clumsily swim up from the bottom, then drift back down to a new location. An excellent pattern for these occasions is the Curled Nymph. The pattern is tied on a bent hook, #4 to #18, depending upon the species to be imitated. Tie in two duck-quill fiber tails halfway down from the bend in the hook. The body is spun fur, ribbed with flat mono. Wrap hen hackle just behind the head and clip it top and bottom. Tie in two latex-sheet wing-pads on the top and the pattern is finished with two antennae of duck-wing quill segments.

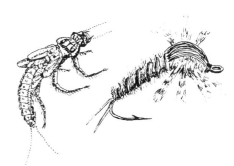

DRIFTING STONEFLY NYMPH

Hook	Curved, #4-#18 3XL Orvis #1510, Tiemco #200
Thread	Dark brown, 3/0 or 6/0, depending upon size
Tail	Two duck-quill fibers that match body color
Body	Spun fur to match species being imitated
Rib	Flat mono
Legs	Speckled hen hackle clipped top and bottom
Wing case	Dark quill segment

Drifting stonefly nymph—adult and artificial

Drifting stonefly

Stonefly nymphs, like all other aquatic invertebrates, must shed their inelastic exoskeletons periodically as they grow. This is called a new *instar*. Each time they undergo this "shedding," their color changes to a much lighter shade. Most species, except the very dark genera, become almost pure white.

At these times, the trout are particularly susceptible to an imitation tied in the Curled Stone pattern, only very light in color. The tails, body, hackle, wing pads, and antennae are very light cream and the ribbing is light yellow. We call the pattern the Albino Stone. Trout prefer this stage if they can get it, much as a smallmouth bass prefers soft-shelled crayfish over hard-shelled crayfish. This pattern is very soft and resilient to the touch and the trout will pick it up gently and actually move off four or five feet while chewing it. There is no problem detecting a strike, because half the line will move upstream. The Albino Stone nymph is very effective during behavioral drift periods.

ALBINO STONEFLY NYMPH

Albino stonefly nymph

Hook	Curved #4-#10, 3XL Orvis #1510, Tiemco #200
Thread	Brown, 3/0
Tail	Gray partridge
Body	Light cream or off-white fur
Rib	Yellow Swannundaze or yellow flat mono
Legs	Gray partridge
Wing case	Clump of tannish cream ostrich herl

Albino stonefly nymph—natural
and artificial

AQUATIC MOTHS

(Order: Lepidoptera)

Aquatic moth

Aquatic moths resemble caddisflies in appearance but their emergence is very different. The pupa develops in a cocoon on the stream bottom, much like a caddis pupa. The adult moth emerges from the pupa *on the bottom* and swims to the surface as a winged insect. Its wings and body have hydrofuge properties, so it does not get wet. After the adults mature, the females dive under water to lay their eggs—so the same imitation works well for both the ascension and the returning egg-layers. Due to this style of emergence and return, the patterns are fished wet.

Patterns

The natural adults are mostly tan, cream, and grayish brown, a little larger than the usual caddis species. They range in size from #10 to #14, whereas most caddis are #14 to #20. Any good caddis-adult pattern in the correct size and color, fished wet, is usually effective. The aquatic moths normally emerge just after dark and the trout do not seem to be particularly selective at these times if the imitation is close to the correct size and shape.

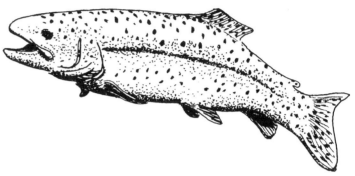

Moth Patterns

Wet-fly hooks—in the sizes #10 to #14 and weighted—should be wrapped with the body in tan or cream spun fur. The hackle should be webby but stiff, two-thirds the length of the body. It should be the same color as the body, tied in reverse style, so the fibers are pointing forward. The wings are two tan or cream hen-hackle tips, flat but V'd out a little.

Aquatic moth (light)

AQUATIC MOTH (LIGHT)

Hook	#10–#14, 2XL, weighted, Orvis #1524 or Tiemco #5262
Thread	Tan or medium brown, 6/0
Body	Tan spun fur
Rib	Fine gold wire
Wing	Tan hen-hackle tips tied flat and V'd out
Hackle	Dark ginger tied reverse style, with the fibers pointing forward

Aquatic moth (dark)

AQUATIC MOTH (DARK)

Aquatic moth (dark)

Hook	#10–#14, 2XL, weighted, Orvis #1524, Tiemco #5262
Thread	Dark brown, 6/0
Body	Grayish-brown spun fur
Rib	Fine gold wire
Wing	Woodchuck or deer hair
Hackle	Brown speckled hen, tied reverse style

MIDGES

(Order: Diptera; Family: Chironomidae)

Midge patterns fall into four categories; two are pupal patterns, one is the emerging adult pattern, and the last is the adult pattern. This is a very diverse family of insects, with over two thousand species identified—and more are being identified every year. The colors can be almost any shade, from black to olive, to red, to tan and cream. They vary widely in size from #14 to #28. When tying these patterns, it is important to know the waters you are fishing, the time of year of the emergence, and the length and color of the insect's body. On slow waters—such as spring creeks, ponds, and lakes—the flies provide an important part of the fishs' diet. Correct size and color are critical for a successful imitation.

Pupal patterns are tied to simulate the naturals ascending from the bottom to the surface, and to imitate the pupa suspended just under the surface, with thorax caught in the film and the body hanging down.

ASCENDING PUPA

Ascending midge pupa

Hook	#14–#28, 1XF st.eye, weighted, Orvis #1637, Tiemco #101
Thread	8/0 to match body color
Swimming paddles	Hackle tip tied short
Body	Spun fur of appropriate color, tied slim
Thorax	Spun fur thicker than body
Spherical gills	Ostrich, emu, or duck-rump feathers

Ascending midge pupa (suspended pattern is the same)

SUSPENDED PUPA

This pattern is the same as the Ascending Pupa but it is not

weighted. A small piece of foam can be substituted for the spherical gills. This will float the fly so that the head is above the surface—and it will also give better visibility.

ONE-HALF-EMERGED ADULT MIDGE

Suspended midge pupa with closed cellfoam wing

Suspended midge pupa with clump of duck-rump feathers for wing

Hook	#14–#28, 1XF st. eye, Orvis #1637, Tiemco #101
Thread	8/0 to match body color
Shuck	Bronze hackle tip, one-third body length
Wings	Two light-gray hackle tips, tied flat and V'd, two-thirds the length of the body

Hackle One or two turns of top-quality cock hackle, clipped top and bottom, equal to the length of the body

Half-emerged adult midge

FULLY EMERGED ADULT MIDGE

This pattern is the same as the half-emerged adult, without the pupal shuck.

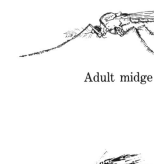

Adult midge

Adult midge

Midge emerger with pupal shuck extending out the back

Midge adult

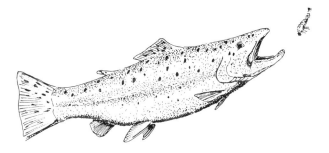

NO-WING PARACHUTE MIDGE
(Under-Midge style)

No-wing midge

Hook	#20–#22, Orvis #1509, Tiemco #100
Thread	8/0, to match body
Body	Spun fur of appropriate color
Hackle	Grizzly, parachute, posted with .015″ round rubber, tied in V style and knotted to hold down hackle

DAMSELFLIES AND DRAGONFLIES

(Order: Odonata)

Dragonfly nymph

These are nymph patterns as the adults emerge on land. The order is widespread on virtually all trout environments. Certain areas, such as Silver Creek in Idaho and many western lakes, have huge populations that provide a major part of the trout's diet.

Damselfly nymph

DRAGONFLY NYMPH

Dragonfly nymph imitation

Dragonfly nymph

Hook	#6–#8, 3XL, weighted, Orvis #1526 or Tiemco #5263
Thread	Dark brown, 3/0
Abdomen	Olive-green or dirty-tan spun fur, tied flat and wide, tapered thin at junction with thorax
Thorax	Fat spun fur, same color as abdomen but not as wide
Hackle	Olive-dyed grizzly hen hackle or brown speckled grouse, tied in behind thorax and clipped top and bottom

DAMSELFLY NYMPH

Damselfly nymph

Damselfly nymph imitation

Hook	#8–#10, 3XL, weighted, Orvis #1526 or Tiemco #5263
Thread	Olive or dark brown, 3/0
Tails	Olive-dyed grizzly hen hackle
Abdomen	Bright-olive or olive-brown spun fur, slim (not flattened)
Rib	Fine gold wire
Thorax	Same as abdomen, only twice as thick
Hackle	Olive-dyed grizzly hen hackle
Wing case	Dark brownish-olive quill segment

CRANEFLIES

(Order: Diptera; Family: Tipulidae)

Cranefly larvae are very large meaty insects, from one to two inches in length; superficially, they resemble a huge, hairless caterpillar. They are found in all types of water, from lakes to fast-flowing streams. Since the larvae are so large, a good imitation can be very successful, especially on selected streams, such as tailwaters, where they are often quite abundant. The Big Horn River in Montana is a prime example. Here, in May and June, the largest trout feed almost selectively on cranefly larvae.

CRANEFLY LARVA

Cranefly larva

Hook	#2–#8, 3XL, weighted, Orvis #1526, Tiemco #5263
Thread	Olive or brown, 6/0
Gills	Gray marabou, very short
Body	Olive to dirty-tan spur fur, tapered to a cigar shape, with guard hairs left in
Rib	Gold wire
Hackle	Olive or brown hen hackle, very short, one or two turns only

Cranefly larva

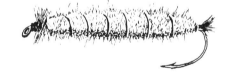

Cranefly larva imitation

There are many different species of craneflies, so if you have a situation where the trout are feeding heavily on them, or you seine the river and find large populations, you should match the size and color of the naturals.

DUCK RUMP PATTERNS

The feathers that we call duck bottoms, or duck rump, come from the underside area of a duck and have unique flotation qualities. Their ability to stay dry is a great asset not only to our waterfowl friends but also to the modern fly tyer, for whom they provide excellent material. We've been using them for some time now for the wings on tiny spinners, mainly for Tricos and *Pseudocloeon*. Recently, however, we've found many other uses for them. They are excellent for imitating both the emerging and fully developed wings of mayflies, especially in the #18 and smaller size range, and they are deadly for caddis and midge patterns. We use them on many types of emergers, for the expanding wing cases on floating nymphs, and even for dubbed bodies. Mixing two or more colors can create some interesting—and killing—effects.

For tiny micro-dun imitations, we normally tie our original no-hackle pattern, with widely split, high-quality cock-hackle tails, spun-fur body, and a clump of duck-rump fibers fanned out waterline to waterline. Paradun-type wings are a little more difficult to fashion because the fibers are so limp and willowy. To get a firm enough post to wrap the parachute hackle on, use a heavier clump or strengthen the wing by adding a piece of .015″ diameter round rubber to the system. Simply straddle the tying thread with the strand of rubber in an inverted V configuration. Then, when you wrap the thread, the rubber will right itself to the normal V position. Take a few more wraps, making sure that the right side of the V is on the front edge of the wing and the left side of the V is on the back edge of the wing. As you wrap the hackle around the entire clump—the wing fibers and two strands of rubber—stretch the rubber during the wrapping process and relax it as you change hands. When you release the rubber after the final wrap of hackle, its diameter more than doubles, creating a compression effect that helps to hold the hackle securely in place. Then merely push your scissors through the wing to cut the rubber barely above the body level. This technique, and slight variations of it, can be used on any parachute tie. It is quicker and much easier than the old "lacing" method. We use it for tying no-wing parachutes and for parachute legs on nymphs. For both of those applications, you can tie an overhand knot with the two rubber ends. This really locks the hackle down.

For emerger wings, tie in a clump of fibers and cut them down to the desired length and shape. Make the clump heavier and longer for a high-floating, high-visibility emerger and make it smaller and shorter for a low in-the-film type. Duck rump does an excellent job of imitating the spherical gills on ascending midge pupae and on suspended midge pupae. It floats the fly with the head up in the proper position and provides good visibility. Duck rump also takes the work out tying microcaddis imitations. One of our favorite styles is to use duck-rump fibers for the entire fly, a dubbed body, and either a conventional or reverse-pull wing. This pattern is easy to tie, it floats like a cork, and it can be skittered beautifully on the surface.

It's easy to find duck-rump feathers. Ask a duck-hunting friend to save them for you, or if you fish a river that has a good population of waterfowl, you'll surely find plenty of feathers along the bank. They can be dyed or easily tinted with a waterproof marker. The feathers float so well naturally that you do not need to apply flotant. In fact, most flotants, especially the popular pastes, will mat the fibers and destroy the high-floating properties of this feather. Scotchguard, however, works very well and will add flotation properties to the other materials in your fly.

TRICO NO-HACKLE DUN

Trico dun with duck-rump wing

Hook	#18–#24, Orvis #1509, Tiemco #100
Thread	Olive, 8/0
Tails	Light-gray cock-hackle fibers

Abdomen	Olive thread
Body	Dark blackish-gray Belgian mole
Wings	White duck-rump fibers

TRICO EMERGER

Trico emerger with duck-rump wing

Hook	#18–#24, Orvis #1509, Tiemco #100
Thread	Olive, 8/0
Tails	Gray partridge
Body	Dark blackish gray Belgian mole
Wings	White duck-rump fibers—clump, short

PSEUDOCLOEON NO-HACKLE DUN

Pseudocloeon dun, no-hackle—with duck-rump wing

Hook	20–24, Orvis #1509, Tiemco #100
Thread	Olive, 8/0
Tails	Light-gray cock-hackle fibers
Body	Bright olive to brownish olive fur
Wings	Off-white to light-gray duck-rump fibers

PSEUDOCLOEON EMERGER

Pseudocloeon emerger with duck-rump feathers

Hook	#20–#24, Orvis #1509, Tiemco #100
Thread	Olive, 8/0
Tails	Gray partridge
Body	Bright olive to brownish olive fur
Wings	Light-gray duck-rump fibers—clump, short

BAETIS PARADUN

Baetis paradun with duck-rump wing

Hook	#18–#20, Orvis #1509, Tiemco #100
Thread	Brown, 8/0
Tails	Olive cock-hackle fibers
Body	Olive to brownish-olive fur
Wings	Gray duck rump, .015″ diameter, round rubber, tied in with wing V style optional
Hackle	Grizzly, parachute

TAN CADDIS PUPA

Hook	#16–#20, Orvis #1509, Tiemco #100
Thread	Dark brown, 8/0
Head	Dark-brown fur, small
Legs	Brown round rubber, .015″ diameter, tied 45° forward
Body	Tan duck-rump fibers, dubbed; fly tied off at tail

GREEN CADDIS PUPA

Hook	#16–#20, Orvis #1509, Tiemco #100

Thread   Dark brown, 8/0

Head   Dark brown to black fur, small

Legs   Gray or brown partridge, tied reverse style

Body   Bright green to dark olive duck-rump fibers, dubbed; fly tied off at tail

TAN CADDIS ADULT

Two caddis adults with duck-rump wings

Hook   #16–#20 Orvis #1509, Tiemco #100

Thread   Brown, 8/0

Body   Tan and olive duck-rump fibers, dubbed

Wing   Tan duck-rump fibers, tied with a reverse pull

GREEN CADDIS ADULT

Hook	#16–#20, Orvis #1509, Tiemco #100
Thread	Olive, 8/0
Body	Green fur
Wing	Gray duck-rump fibers

PALE MORNING DUN FLOATING NYMPH

Floating mayfly nymph

Hook	#16–#20, Orvis #1509, Tiemco #100
Thread	Dark brown, 8/0
Tails	Merganser
Body	Brown fur
Wing case	Yellowish-tan duck-rump fibers
Legs	Merganser

6

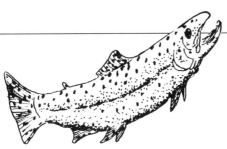

Techniques for Fishing below the Surface

THE angler must learn two skills in order to be consistently successful. First, he must learn how to select the right fly and, second, he must learn how to make the proper presentation. A fly fisherman armed with the perfect fly doesn't have a prayer if he can't present it properly. On the other hand, the world's greatest fly caster will not be successful if the wrong fly is attached to his leader. Pattern and presentation go hand in hand. Each is half of the magical formula for success.

We feel, however, that proper presentation is the foundation of fly fishing. After all, someone can *give* you the right fly but no one can cast for you! Accurate casting and precise line manipulation must be mastered if you are to be successful on the stream. These physical skills can easily be learned with a little practice. In this chapter, we'll cover the techniques required to fish nymphs and emergers below the surface; then, in the following chapter, you'll learn how we fish in the film and on the surface.

Our tackle is pretty basic. We prefer lightweight graphite rods that are eight to nine feet long and handle #4 or #5 weight-forward, high-visibility floating fly lines. Generous-sized rod guides are important to good shooting, mending, and feeding. A high-floating, bright-colored line aids tremendously in line manipulation and control, not to mention the mental confidence it provides. The better you see your system on the water, the quicker you'll learn these techniques and improve your efficiency. Fly fishing is a "visual improvement" sport—you've got to *see* your mistakes in order to make corrections. Even the butt sections of the leaders we use are dyed chartreuse for better visibility. This is a very helpful feature, especially when fishing with nymphs, wet flies, and emergers. It acts as an indicator to give you more precise visual contact with your fly and allows for quicker strike detection. Another important feature of the leaders we prefer is that the butts are made of flat monofilament. This results in tighter loops, better turnover, and less kinking. For the bulk of our fishing, leaders in the nine to twelve-foot range are about right, but for deep nymphing and critical dry-fly situations, leaders up to twenty feet long may be necessary.

Our goal in the following pages is to teach you how to fish the hatch from "bottom to top." Eventually, with a reasonable amount of practice, you should be able to fish your artificial fly—whether nymph, emerger, wet fly, or dry fly—at any depth from any angle on the stream. To accomplish this goal, you'll need to master the four basic casts: *straight line, crooked line (slack), angled line (reach),* and *curve*—along with the line-manipulation techniques of stripping, feeding, and mending. Just an hour of practice every day for a few weeks should put you well on your way to becoming a proficient caster. Unfortunately, there are no short cuts; you must pay your dues on the casting field.

Let's start with the techniques required to allow your fly to drift drag-free along the stream bottom. We'll begin with shallow water, approximately one to two feet, then cover deeper water, approximately two to four feet, and finally very deep runs, four feet deep and over.

A shallow, relatively slow-moving riffle is the best place to start, especially if you're a beginner. Use a lightly weighted fly tied to a 5X high-visibility leader that is nine to twelve feet long. Make the first cast directly upstream. Since you're casting into the same lane of current you're standing in, your line, leader, and fly will all be drifting toward you at basically the same speed—so a fancy presentation cast is not necessary. A normal straight-line cast will do. As soon as the fly hits the water, apply the "control system"; this means that you should put the line over the index finger of your rod hand, lower the rod tip to the water, and strip in the slack. Strip the line as straight as possible *but not tight enough to drag the fly!* There should be just enough slack to keep drag from forming. With this tight low-rod system, you're in a great position to set the hook and make a clean pickup for the next cast. If your fly is not drifting deep enough, cast a little farther upstream or put more slack in the cast, or both, and strip a tad slower. If you're hanging up on the bottom too much, cast a little straighter and strip a tad faster.

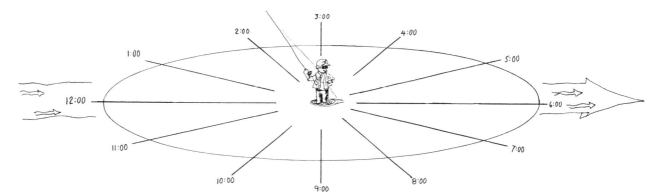

The clock system

Now, let's start working in a clockwise direction, making casts at various angles. If we call our first upstream cast the 12:00 o'clock position, let's make one at the 1:30 position. At this angle, we'll be slicing across varying currents, so let's throw more slack line. This can be done in a variety of ways. The easiest is merely to aim your cast high over the horizon and then quickly, but smoothly, lower the rod tip to the water. You can also pull back with the line hand just as the loop straightens or wiggle the rod horizontally with quick movements of your wrist. Use the method that works best for you. As the fly hits the water, again apply the "control system." Put the line over your finger, lower the rod tip to the water, and strip in any slack that forms.

You'll find that at this angle—in fact, at *any* angle other than directly upstream—an additional step must be added to the "control system." It's called "go with the flow," which means that you follow the drifting line with your rod tip. If you don't follow along at the speed of the current, drag will form almost immediately. This step is a must for holding off drag as long as possible.

As a result of our slack-line cast and "go with the flow" movement, the fly should be moving naturally along the bottom by the time it drifts even with our position on the stream. At about this time, however, the line will be forming a large bow that will create drag on the fly. Just before this happens, carefully throw an upstream mend; this will add slack to the system and extend the natural drift. Depending upon how much line you're using and how far you want to extend the drift, you can mend two, three, or more times. Eventually, the line will tighten and the fly will swing up to the surface.

Next, continuing in a clockwise direction, fish directly toward the bank. This is called the 3:00 o'clock position and, at this angle, you'll be casting across the maximum number of varying currents. More effort will be required to fight drag; so, instead of the slack-line cast, use a reach cast, which will extend the natural drift even farther. For the right-handed caster, this is called a "cross-body reach" and, once mastered, will become your deadliest weapon in fighting drag. The mechanics of this all-important cast will be covered more thoroughly in the next chapter, "Techniques for Fishing at the Surface"—that is, fishing the dry fly—but basically, it is a method of laying the line on the water at the proper angle to get the longest possible float. During the cast, with smooth, even power, you must learn to change the direction of the rod 90° and "paint" the line on the water. For our 3:00 o'clock position, the fly will be delivered straight toward the bank but the rod will be pointed directly at 12:00 o'clock at the completion of the cast. As soon as the fly hits the water, lower the rod tip and "go with the flow." This will keep the pressure off your nymph, allowing it to sink quickly in the shallow water and drift naturally along the bottom. Mending can be added as needed to reduce drag buildup.

To fish the downstream quadrant effectively, from approximately the 4:30 to 7:30 positions on the clock, mastery of the slack-line cast and how to feed line is imperative. You should be able to throw varying amounts of slack with pinpoint accuracy and feed line out through the guides quickly and smoothly. For the right-handed caster, the most efficient method of feeding is to transfer line from your left hand to your right index finger, which induces excess line into the system; then "bounce" your rod. The cadence is "left, right, *bounce*—left, right, bounce." If done properly, the line will literally "fly" out of the guides without affecting the natural drift of the artificial. This technique will sink your fly to the bottom very quickly, especially in shallow runs and riffles. Actually, stack mending, which you'll learn later when we start fishing in deeper water, is based on this principle of keeping the leader and line directly upstream of the fly. In fact, when fishing slow to medium-speed water less than two feet deep, you may have to increase slightly the tension of feeding to prevent snagging and hanging up on the bottom.

Continuing clockwise, let's fish what we call the "right bank quadrant," from 7:30 to 10:30 on our imaginary stream clock. This, of course, is similar to the "left bank quadrant" except that the current is moving from right to left. For this situation, a reach cast, this time to the right, followed by the "go with the flow" routine and mending should allow our wet fly or nymph to sink quickly and glide along the stream bottom in a natural manner. Now we are back to the "upstream quadrant," 10:30 to 1:30, where we originally started.

To fish water that's a little deeper, approximately two to four feet, we can basically use the same techniques we used for shallower water, with a few variations. First, we might want to lengthen the leader. This makes casting a bit more difficult but allows the fly to sink quicker and deeper. Adding two or three feet can make quite a difference. Second, we'll be doing more mending. Drag builds up faster in the deeper water so we'll be repositioning our line more often. Learn to make your mends with super-quick flips of the wrist. This will get you ready for stack mending.

At this point, we'll also start adding weight to the system. There are a variety of ways to go. Though you can add more weight to the fly by using heavier hooks and wrapping lead on the shank as an underbody, heavy flies tend to hang up on the bottom; and they do not drift as naturally as lighter ones. Too much lead used in the tying process can also make a fly look "pregnant" and totally out of proportion. It's better to use split shot or lead sleeves, each of which has advantages and disadvantages. Shot is easy to put on but has the nasty habit of flying off your leader, always at an inopportune time. Lead sleeves must be threaded on, but once in place cast smoother, snag less on rocks, and can be used over and over.

There are a couple of important points to remember when using lead. Use just enough weight to match the technique you are using, so that your fly will drift along the bottom naturally. A system that is too heavy will constantly hang up on rocks and snags. This causes great frustration and really eats into your effective fishing time. Your normal "dry-fly casting stroke" will have to change a little. You must slow down a bit and make your loops wider. The greater the weight, the slower the stroke and the wider the loops. Quick motions and tight "candy canes" will only result in lots of tangles.

Once you're accustomed to handling the longer, weighted leader, try the "clock" routine in two to four feet of water. With a little practice, you should be able to make long, drag-free drifts along the bottom of the stream.

Now you're ready to learn the ultimate technique for nymphing in deep water and fast currents.

Stack mending is a method that utilizes your casting skills, instead of weights, to fish your fly effectively in the deepest, most difficult runs. It is based on the principle that you must keep as much of the leader and line as possible directly upstream from the fly during the drift. Lanes of current that are adjacent to the lane of current the fly is in are normally flowing at varying speeds. If the line and leader are allowed to drift in those lanes, the difference in speed causes tension to build up in the system. This, of course, creates drag, or pressure, on the fly and prevents it from sinking deep.

The trick is to learn how to manipulate your line and leader so that they remain straight upstream from your fly for as long as possible during the drift. By keeping them out of neighboring lanes of current, all parts of the system—fly, leader, and line—cruise along at the same speed. This eliminates tension and, as a result, your artificial sinks and drifts in a natural manner.

Let's go through the step-by-step procedure for stack mending. First, establish the location where you want your fly to be drifting along the bottom. This is where you think fish are holding and is called the "primary target." For starters, position yourself twenty feet upstream and ten feet across-stream from this spot. Next, select a "secondary target"—the point you must cast to that will allow enough time for your nymph to sink to the stream bottom. This will take a little experience, or trial and error, to get right.

Make a straight-line cast four or five feet beyond the secondary target. Immediately raise your rod to slide the fly back to the target. This movement breaks the surface tension, allows the leader and fly to start sinking, puts the rod in the correct position for the first mend, and also creates the necessary slack that you'll "shoot" in behind the fly. Now, start the shooting process. With quick snaps of your wrist, shoot tight little loops of line right in behind the fly, stacking them one on top of the other. Each mend induces a small amount of line into the system. As the fly approaches the primary target, remove most of the slack so you can detect strikes and set the hook quickly.

Stack mending is one of the more difficult presentation techniques to master, but once you get the hang of it, you'll be able to fish deep runs and fast currents that you always avoided in the past. Also, you'll be amazed at how easily you can get long drag-free drifts in shallow runs and riffles with totally *unweighted* flies.

So far, we've covered techniques that give drag-free drifts along the bottom of the stream. We discussed how to handle various depths of water and how to make presentations from every possible angle. Now let's cover what we can do at the end of the drift. First of all, with each of the techniques, the drift can be extended by mending and feeding. Sometimes that extra few feet of drift will buy us a strike. Also, the way that we manipulate the fly at the end of the drift can be very important. Quite often, you have to experiment to see what the fish want at any particular time.

Sometimes, what we call "dead-rise" or "dead-swing" works just fine. Nothing could be easier. Just hold the rod still and let the fly swing. If the fly is drifting in line with the rod tip—in other words, straight below you—it will speed up and rise through the currents vertically. If the fly was drifted well off to the side, or if you mended to the side, it will not only rise but swing laterally. Each of these retrieves simulates the movement of certain aquatic insects, mainly caddis pupae and some of the fast-swimming mayfly nymphs. The addition of motion—from a subtle twitch to an active swimming movement—

can create even more realism. You should experiment with various stripping and rod-vibrating techniques, both singularly and in combination. Then, learn to apply them at all depths and at all angles of the clock.

Here are some of our favorite retrieves and how we use them:

- **Strip 'n Bounce.** A super-fast one-inch strip coupled with a quick bounce of the rod—imparts great action to wiggle nymphs.

- **Vibrate 'n Lift.** All done with the rod hand; quick vibrations in the wrist as the rod is lifted overhead—excellent for rising caddis pupae.

- **Lift 'n Drop.** Also done with rod hand; lift slowly and vibrate, then drop quickly—works well with soft hackles.

- **Constant Speed.** Strip with *both* hands—hand over hand; best in slower water with weighted cranefly larva.

- **Figure-8 'n Bounce.** Standard figure-8 nymph retrieve done erratically, coupled with bounce of rod—big nymphs like *Hexagenia*.

- **Mend 'n Follow.** Remember that the fly goes where the line goes, so if you can mend the line in a certain direction or to a certain spot, the fly will follow when you make the retrieve—great for swimming weighted stonefly nymphs toward the bank or any nymph broadside to the current.

Remember that strikes during a retrieve normally come on a tight line, so be prepared to let the line slide a little so you don't break off or pull the hook out of the trout's mouth.

Another important point in nymphing is to try to maintain a constant "tension factor"; this is the curve the line makes as it falls from the rod tip to the water. It is much easier to detect strikes if you keep this curve constant. To do this, merely raise and lower the tip of your rod; as the system drifts toward you, the rod tip must be raised to keep the curve constant, and as the system drifts away from you, the rod tip must be lowered.

The "tension factor" is actually a measure of slack in the line and leader, and it takes a lot of visual concentration on this system to detect a strike. To alleviate this problem, many fly fishermen, mostly beginners, fish with an "indicator," which can be anything that floats well and has high visibility—a piece of yarn, closed-cell foam, another fly, even a small cork bobber. It is attached to the leader above the nymph, or nymphs, at the correct distance to cover the water being fished best, usually two to six feet. Most anglers who use this system will tell you they do so because it enables them, visually, to detect strikes better. This is a factor but the *real* advantage is that it gives them a great mode of presentation yet requires very little effort or skill. The indicator mechanically does the same thing stack mending does without having to spend all of those hours learning one of the most difficult techniques in fly fishing.

Another method of fishing nymphs deep is what we call the "tight line" technique. It is based on the fact that nothing sinks like a piece of fine monofilament with lead on it. This method is most effective when you can stand only a few feet away from the fish you're trying to catch, preferably in water that is turbulent enough to mask your presence. By using a long, fine leader with the correct amount of lead attached a foot or two above the nymph, you simply plop the fly upstream and let it bounce along the bottom in front of you. These short drifts are repeated time after time without any fly line ever touching the water. The real key here is to select the right amount of lead for the current being fished. You need just enough to bounce barely along the bottom but not enough to hang up. This is not the most exciting way to fish but it can be deadly once you get on to it. Because of all the weight and tension in the system you must be quick to set the hook.

7

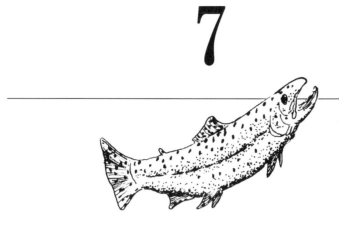

Techniques for Fishing at the Surface

NOW comes the fun part—fishing up on top. Even though underwater techniques may be the deadliest over the long haul, nothing matches the excitement of fishing at the surface of the stream. Everything is visual: the feeding fish, the drifting artificial, and the take. You can see it all happening right in front of you, in wonderful panorama. The strike, especially, is probably the most exciting moment in fishing. Many of our most wonderful angling memories center around that precise moment when a trout of seemingly gargantuan proportions exploded at the surface.

This visual aspect of fishing on top not only adds to the enjoyment of the sport but also makes the fisherman's job a little easier. It practically eliminates the need to read the water because you'll be able to see the fish as they feed on naturals that are drifting in the film. By having actual targets to cast at, you can easily determine your accuracy with the fly and check the quality of your drag-free float; this, of course, is the problem fishing nymphs and wet flies—in fact, any subsurface fly. Since you normally can't see the fish, your fly, or the end of your leader, you might guess where the trout is holding and hope that your presentation was accurate and natural. This is why many anglers are poor nymphers. With everything out of sight below the stream's surface, they lose the mental confidence it takes to be successful.

To fish on top, we'll basically be using the same casts and line-manipulation techniques that we used for fishing under the surface. You'll need at least a good working knowledge of the basic presentation casts: straight line, slack line, reach, and curve, plus the ability to strip, feed, and mend efficiently. A major difference will be the addition of skittering, which will replace stack mending as a specialty technique. We'll be using the same tackle, with nine to twelve-foot leaders, although the flies will be lighter and there will be no weight in the system. Also, with subsurface fishing, we had to be concerned with varying currents in *both* the horizontal and vertical directions. We must worry only about the varying lateral currents when we fish on the surface.

As mentioned in the preceeding chapter, it is imperative that you learn how to present your fly properly from any position on the stream. The "clock" concept is the most helpful we have found for learning the various presentation techniques. Picture yourself standing in the middle of the stream at the center of an imaginary clock. Straight upstream is 12:00 o'clock and straight downstream is 6:00 o'clock. Starting at 12:00 o'clock, keep rotating clockwise and see if you can make the right presentation to get the longest possible float at each angle of the clock.

We used the clock reference in the previous chapter on nymphing and now we'll repeat and refine it a bit. Its use for deep nymphing, at least for beginners, is somewhat limited. For dry fly, however, you can use the concept to improve your presentation techniques quickly. You'll discover that your relationship to the current will change with each position as you rotate through the various angles of the clock. As this relationship changes, you'll have to employ different methods to fight drag. Eventually, when you've mastered all of the individual techniques, you can combine them, playing them off one another, to achieve some incredibly long drag-free floats.

Let's go through the eight major positions of the clock (every

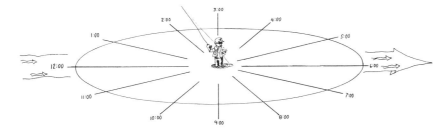

The clock system

45°) and discuss the best presentation techniques to use at each position, starting straight upstream and working clockwise. Assume a right-handed caster.

12:00 o'clock   Straight upstream with the current moving directly at you. Since you're casting into the same lane of current you're standing in (it's all going at the same speed) use a straight-line cast. Immediately put the line over your right index finger, lower the rod tip to the water, and strip in the slack that forms as the fly floats toward you. Keep stripping the line as tightly as possible *without* dragging the fly. With the low rod tip and tight line, you're in a great position to set the hook and also to make the pickup for the next cast. In really fast water, where it's difficult to strip fast enough to keep the slack out, use the roll pickup. If you're throwing to a spooky fish straight upstream, use a reach cast so that the line and leader will not pass over him.

1:30   Upstream 45° to left bank, current moving left to right. A slack-line cast will give you a fairly good natural float but the cross-body reach cast (to the left) is better. After the cast is made, apply the "control system"—line over the finger, lower the rod, and "go with the flow" (follow the drifting line with your rod tip). Automatically apply the control system to each technique. Mending can also be added to extend the drift.

3:00 o'clock   Straight to the left bank with the current moving left to right. In this and the 9:00 o'clock position you are normally covering the greatest number of varying currents. A slack-line cast with feeding works fairly well but the cross-body reach cast (to the left) with feeding is much better. You'll get at least twice the amount of drag-free float with the same effort. The reach lays the line well upstream from the fly at a very steep angle. In this position, it takes much longer for the line and leader to bow downstream and create drag on the fly.

4:30   Downstream 45° to the left bank, current moving left to right. The most popular position of all for the right-handed caster. The cross-body reach cast (to the left) with feeding is definitely the cast here. Unbelievably long drag-free floats are possible at this angle. Also, the mode of presentation is excellent as the fly comes into the trout's window ahead of the leader. At this angle, however, the hook must be set slowly and gently to avoid missed strikes and breakoffs.

6:00 o'clock   Straight downstream with the current moving away. In this direction you need lots of slack and you must learn to throw it with good accuracy. As soon as the cast hits the water, start bouncing the rod to feed line quickly. Long floats are possible at this angle; and it is an excellent mode of presentation. To keep from "lining" specific risers, add a reach to the slack.

7:30   Downstream 45° to the right bank, current moving right to left. Another "favorite" position. The slack-line cast, reach cast, or curve cast (to the left) with feeding are excellent; but the best presentation cast is the reach-curve cast with feeding. The reach is to the right and the curve is to the left. The same long floats you get at the 4:30 position are possible, but with a little less accuracy and control. This angle will also help you present the fly in the trout's window before the leader.

9:00 o'clock Straight to the right bank, current moving right to left. The reach-curve cast followed by feeding line is best for the longest natural float. This is exactly the same presentation that we used at the 7:30 position. By coupling the reach and the curve casts, you can lay more line and leader directly upstream from the fly than you can with any of the other techniques.

10:30 Upstream 45° to the right bank, current moving right to left. A slack-line cast will produce a good float and a reach cast (to the right) is even better: but the best drift of all is achieved by using the reach curve cast, where the line curves to the left. Mending will also extend the float.

Slack-line Cast

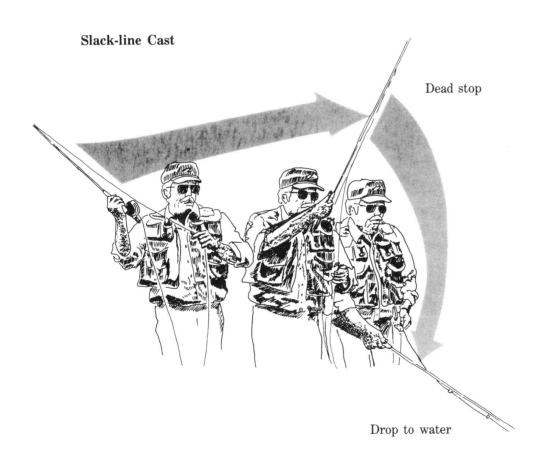

Dead stop

Drop to water

In order to improve your presentation skills, we recommend you practice "fishing the clock" as often as possible, either on the stream or right in your own back yard.

The real nuts and bolts of presentation is learning to master three very important casts: controlled slack-line cast, cross-body reach cast, and positive curve cast. To improve your skill level in performing these casts, we'll discuss each one and give you some tips on how to improve and refine them.

Supposedly, one of the first casts you learn and one of the easiest to throw is the slack-line cast; yet we are always surprised to see how few fly fishermen utilize this cast with any degree of accuracy or control. If you really have this cast down pat, you should be able to form even serpentines all the way from rod tip to fly, to be accurate in windy conditions (within reason), and to be able to tuck your fly up under branches hanging three to four feet over the stream bank. If this isn't what you can actually do, then here's what to practice: Throw a wide front loop aimed high over the horizon and immediately touch your rod tip to the water. The line should "puddle" evenly all the way from your rod tip to the fly. If it doesn't, you either aimed your loop too low, didn't drop your rod tip to the water quickly enough, or both.

As soon as the "puddling" becomes second nature, start pulling the line with your left hand (for right-handers) just before the line straightens over the water; you may have to experiment a little with the quickness and timing of the pull. Your hand should be snapped with a short six-inch movement toward your thigh. If you pull outward, you'll find that your hand will move two feet or more and the timing necessary to make the line "jump back" will be destroyed. Once you've mastered the wrist snap you can start tightening and lowering your loop, which will allow you to handle the wind and place your fly under overhanging obstructions.

The reach cast, without question, *is the deadliest of all the presentation casts*. It produces much longer, more predictable drag-free floats than the slack-line cast and can be cast with more accuracy and authority than the curve cast. It is far superior to mending because it is "off and running" and working for you the second it hits the water. There's no need to adjust the line and leader.

Both reaches, right and left, are important, but the cross-body reach (to the left for a right-hander) is the most effective.

The Reach Cast

One continuous sweeping motion

Since the cross-body version is a one-way movement of the arm and wrist, it has more control, is more accurate, fights the wind better, and is much easier to tuck under overhanging obstructions.

The object of the reach cast is to lay the line either upstream or down (depending on the current) from the fly in a position that provides the longest possible drift. Normally, but not always, the line is laid upstream from the fly. Also, the more parallel the line is to the current, the longer the drag-free float; and, conversely, the more perpendicular the line is to the current, the shorter the float.

For the basic reach cast, throw an extremely wide loop with your rod in the vertical plane, keeping the backcast high and the front cast low. The vertical rod keeps the fly from hooking, a serious problem for beginners, and the extreme forward tilt will help in mastering accuracy and control, especially in the wind. Wide loops mean a slow wrist and that is what you need to learn the reach cast. In fact, the wrist hardly works at all, at least in the learning process.

During the delivery, using a slow wrist and *even* power, "paint" the line on the water as you change the direction of your rod tip 90° to the left. As the fly hits the water, you

The Reach Curve Cast

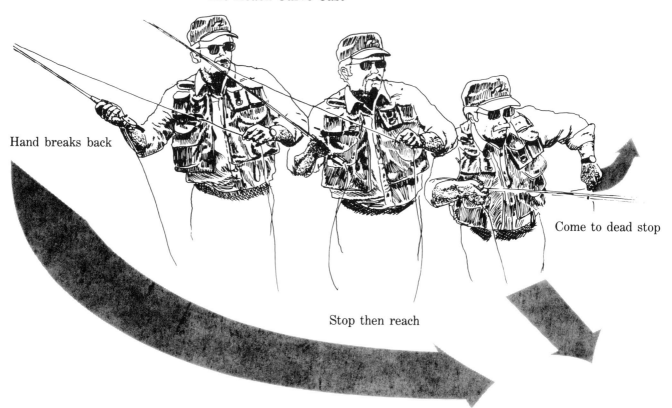

Hand breaks back

Come to dead stop

Stop then reach

The Curve Cast

Hand breaks back

Come to dead stop

should be reaching as far as possible in the direction of the reach. Keep your thumb on top of the cork during the entire cast.

If you're still having trouble, here's a dynamite exercise that should put the final touch on your technique: Combine two individual movements—a straight-line cast with a dragging motion. First, make a straight-line cast 45° to the right of the target. Then, swing your casting arm to the left, dragging the line into the proper position. Gradually, start the dragging motion sooner and sooner until the two movements are blended into one.

Work on the reach cast until you have it mastered; it will pay *tremendous* dividends on the stream. It won't be long until you'll be thinking of *angles* on almost every cast—"which way should I lay the line on the water to get the longest possible float?" Actually, the very best application of the cross-body reach (for right-handed casters) is to fish downstream to the left bank, which is the 4:30 position on the clock. For the left-handed caster, it would be fishing downstream to the right bank, or the 7:30 position.

The positive curve is another deadly weapon you should have in your arsenal of presentation techniques. It produces even longer drag-free drifts than the reach cast—that's the good news. The bad news is that curves are harder to learn and very difficult to control. They require more "touch" and "finesse" than any of the other casts.

For the right-handed caster, the positive curve hooks around to the left. The key to throwing it is to cast a tight loop from a flat sidearm plane. Here's where a super-quick snap of the wrist is necessary on the final delivery cast. This will not only straighten the line but will actually reverse it, or flip it around to the left, putting the fly well downstream of the line.

There are a couple of things you can do to give the cast an extra "kick." Pull back slightly with your rod hand just as the candy cane is about to straighten, or apply a subtle pull with your line hand, or do both at the same time.

For right-handers, the positive curve is the preferred cast to use when fishing the right bank, from the 10:30 to 7:30 positions of the clock. It is deadly because it is delivered from a low sidearm angle, allowing you to slice your fly under branches, bushes, and other overhanging objects. Of course, when you learn to add the reach to your curves, you'll extend your floats even farther. An accurate reach-curve cast is the ultimate weapon for most situations.

Perfect these important presentation techniques and you'll be well on your way to becoming a master fly fisherman.

The addition of one more technique will make you an even more successful fisherman when fishing a hatch. Once you've mastered the art of achieving drag-free floats, then you should learn how to skitter a fly, or give it movement—not just any movement, but the natural, lifelike motion of real insects. This may sound simple, but it takes a lot of practice. Anyone can move their fly on the water with fast stripping and by jerking their rod around, but until you develop some finesse, you'll end up either drowning the fly or pulling it clear out of the water.

Skittering is normally thought of as being a no-hatch, searching type of technique. We find, however, that it also works well when the hatch is on and the fish are rising. If you watch the water closely during an emergence, especially on a warm, breezy day, you'll notice all kinds of movement on the surface. Insects are continually skittering, twitching, taking off, landing, and generally fluttering about, so why not imitate this phenomena. The trick is to make your artificial act like a natural.

The first step is to be sure that your entire system floats as high as possible on the water. To make your flies float higher and last longer, dip them in Scotchguard the night before and let them air dry on a paper towel until morning. For a really quick job, put them in a wire strainer, spray them with Scotchguard (outside, of course) and then dry them with a hair dryer. Either way, this will waterproof your flies and also make them impervious to fish slime. Put them in your fly box and then, when you're ready to use each one, use Albolene or your favorite paste-type flotant. Use it sparingly, but take time to rub it in evenly on all parts of the fly.

Also, and this is really important, be sure to put flotant on your tippet and line each time you change flies—and sometimes more often. We even carry a special, heavier consistency, paste-type flotant that is used just for the leader and line. Leaders with flat monofilament butt sections float, and skitter, better than any other. Braided-butt leaders don't skitter well because of all the water buildup that occurs in the voids between the braided fibers.

The actual instructions for skittering are quite simple: just

Skittering

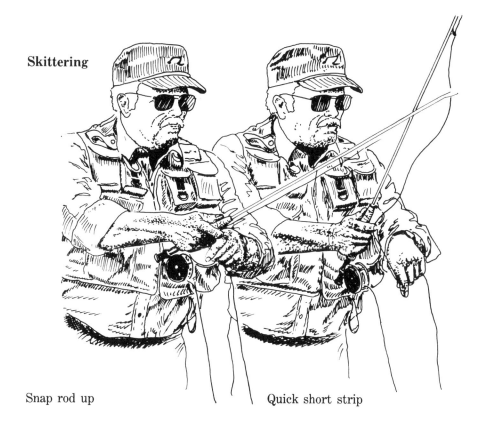

Snap rod up   Quick short strip

strip and twitch the rod—but the "touch" required to make
your movements look natural takes a bit of practice. The problem is learning just how much pressure to put on the fly to get
the right result. As you fish at different angles on the stream,
3:00 o'clock, 6:00 o'clock, and so forth, you must vary the speed
of stripping and the energy put into vibrating the rod. Skittering cross-stream, at the 3:00 o'clock and 9:00 o'clock positions,
is probably the best place to start. After the cast is made, elevate the rod and make tiny, quick-paced, four-inch strips with
your line hand. At precisely the same moment you snap your
left wrist *down* to make the strip, snap your right wrist *up* to
vibrate the rod. By snapping both wrists apart at exactly the
same time with very short, sudden movements, your fly should
"come to life" on the water. Learn to reduce your wrist movements down to one inch or less, and you'll be astounded how
realistically your fly will look as it dances, flutters, and skims
across the currents.

Practice in every direction until you can handle all angles of
the clock. You'll find that skittering into the upstream quadrant (10:30 to 1:30) not only improves the hooking angle but
also gives you some very realistic and controlled movements.

Skittering is very effective on fish that are feeding in places where drag-free floats are difficult to achieve. Backwaters, eddies, and reverse currents are challenging areas that usually harbor big trout, and the easiest way to get their attention is to skitter a fly right over their heads. This method is especially deadly when floating a river where you only have one shot at the fish.

Another way of utilizing the skittering technique is to alternate it with drag-free floats. We call this method "changing lanes." Here's the way it works using the 3:00 o'clock position: Make a reach cast near the bank, lower your rod, "go with the flow," and watch your system closely. As the bow in the line forms and drag is about to begin, elevate the rod and skitter the fly toward you two to three feet, then quickly drop the rod tip to the water. You'll notice that lifting the rod took the bow out of the line and dropping it quickly induced enough slack to give you another drag-free float. This can be repeated two, three, or more times; it allows you to cover a maximum amount of water with one cast. You'll be surprised how often the fish prefer the skitter to the drag-free mode. Changing lanes works best when all the fish are "up" in a large pool.

Multi-Fly System

If you like skittering, you'll find dancing two or three flies on the water even more exciting. Due to the increased air resistance and the greater possibility of tangling, casting is a little tougher, but the rewards are well worth the extra effort. There are several advantages to the multi-fly system, the first being that it allows you to test two or three flies at one time. During an emergence of Pale Morning Duns, for example, you can try quite a variety of combinations to see which pattern works best.

The multi-fly system. All knots are swirle knots

If fully emerged duns are on the water and you can definitely observe that they are being taken, rig up three of your favorite high-floating subimago patterns. One of our favorite combinations in this situation would be a gray/yellow no-hackle dun, a gray/yellow paradun, and a gray/yellow V-hackle dun, sometimes called a thorax dun. If it's a warm, windy day and the duns are fluttering and skittering about, you might want to substitute a Light Cahill or similar-style pattern for one of the flies. If the fish are feeding on the surface but you can't tell if they're taking duns or not, then an excellent Tri-Fly System to use is a no-hackle dun, a duck-quill emerger, and a floating nymph. We use this threesome quite often when fishing spring creeks. For those times when it's obvious that the trout are *not* taking the natural duns but are feeding on the surface, try combinations that simulate emergers, floating nymphs, and trapped or stillborn duns. A good bet for this situation would be a dun/tan duck-quill emerger, a yellow/brown floating nymph, and a gray/yellow trapped dun pattern. Before the actual rise to the PMDs starts, fishing deep can be quite effective; so a good combination here would be a drifting nymph and a wiggle nymph. To minimize casting and tangling problems, we find that it's better to put the wiggle nymph at the terminal end of the system.

The use of more than one fly can also be deadly during an emergence of caddisflies. A favorite trick is to fish an adult pattern, such as a hen caddis or elk-hair caddis, as the upper, or lead, fly, and a caddis pupa as the dropper fly. Adding a third fly, the emerging adult caddis, in between this duo gives you even more potential. The multi-fly system can also be valuable when several species are hatching at the same time. During the early season in Michigan, for example, both the Hendrickson and the Little Black Caddis can be on the water simultaneously. Some fish seem to be keyed on the large mayfly, while others are zero-ed in on the tiny caddis. You have a definite advantage if you're fishing both patterns.

The ability to fish more than a single fly allows you to test one artificial against another at the same time. This is important when you're checking out a new creation from your tying bench. Since conditions are constantly changing on a trout stream, the evaluation of competing patterns is much more meaningful when they are fished together.

With more than one fly attached to your leader, you can

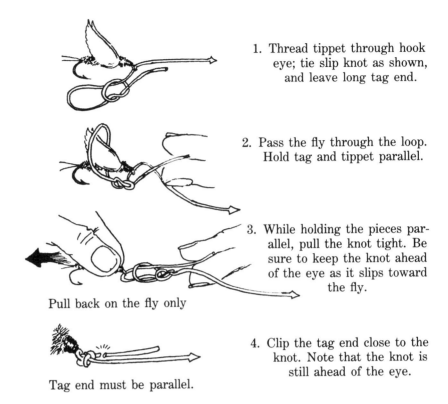

1. Thread tippet through hook eye; tie slip knot as shown, and leave long tag end.

2. Pass the fly through the loop. Hold tag and tippet parallel.

3. While holding the pieces parallel, pull the knot tight. Be sure to keep the knot ahead of the eye as it slips toward the fly.

Pull back on the fly only

4. Clip the tag end close to the knot. Note that the knot is still ahead of the eye.

Tag end must be parallel.

cover more water and this can be a very important factor, especially when the fishing is slow. On a really "tough" day, probably no more than ten percent of the fish in the river are candidates to take your fly. In order to have much of a chance of catching any trout at all, you have to cover a lot of water. With this in mind, it is obvious that two flies can cover twice the area and three flies can cover three times the area of water fished—*if* you fish them properly. The key is to keep the line and leader perpendicular to the current. In this position, the widest possible segment of current can be covered.

Remember: On a slow day, it is important to cover as much water as possible. In fact, a good principle to keep in mind is, "When the fishing is fast, move slow, and when the fishing is slow, move fast." In other words, when fish are feeding all around you, move slowly and fish them thoroughly, and when things are tough, cover lots of water.

One of the most important advantages of the multi-fly system is that it provides tremendous skittering possibilities. Due to the buoying effect of the lead fly, the fly on the end skitters beautifully. It seems to gather more momentum and gyrates all over the place. As the lead fly swings one way, the tail fly goes the other. These gyrations can be emphasized even more by using what we call "alternating riffling hitches." If you're using three dries, riffle hitch the first and third fly on the same side and the middle fly on the opposite side. This rigging puts everything out of line and creates lots of movement. With or without the riffle hitches, more than one fly on the water seems to excite the trout and makes them more aggressive.

Knots are very critical when using the multi-fly technique. We don't want any weak links in the system, so we use the new Swirle Knot for all of the connections. The Swirle has the highest strength of any fly-fishing knot; it is easy to use with our rigging method; and it does not inhibit hooking. We simply tie one fly directly to the other, making the attachment on the bend of the hook with the Swirle Knot. This arrangement keeps all the flies in a straight line, reduces tangling, and can be assembled very quickly.

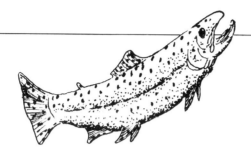

Coda

IN the previous chapters we have explained the methods of locomotion that various orders of trout-stream insects use to propel themselves to the surface at hatch time and during invertebrate drift. We then detailed how they molt and emerge from the larval and pupal cuticle—a time at which they are especially vulnerable to trout predation. Then we suggested imitations that can be fished to simulate the natural movement of the insects, plus techniques for casting and manipulation of the artificials.

It is crucial for the angler to have thorough knowledge of the swimming or crawling motions of the immature insects. Each order exhibits different habits, so if you are fishing to a caddis hatch you must manipulate the artificial as a caddis pupa or caddis emergent, not as an immature mayfly. These insects do not resemble each other while ascending to the surface film. Their actions at the surface are also dissimilar. All orders of aquatic insects possess their own idiosyncrasies and to fish these orders you must first be able to recognize the type of insect that is active, exactly how they get to the surface, and

113

the manner in which they behave once they get there.

We hope this book will serve as a guide to how the various trout-stream insects act before and during the hatch. The next step, after absorbing this information, is to select an appropriate artificial that not only possesses the appearance of the natural when swimming, crawling, drifting, and emerging, but can also be manipulated to simulate the very different swimming motions of the pupae and nymphs. We have suggested some patterns in Chapter 5 that we believe fulfill all these requirements, and certainly many more ties will be invented by resourceful fly tyers. But tyers should keep in mind that patterns should be kept as simple as possible. No one is going to use a pattern very often that is intricate and takes an hour to construct—except perhaps a few anglers who dress their own, and have lots of time on their hands.

Some of the synthetic fibers lend themselves to innovation. An example: When imitating the nymphal or pupal cuticle being extruded from the rear of the emerging insect, a translucent material with a shiny, brassy color is needed for caddis. Most caddis shucks have this characteristic; and there are many synthetics that make a good match. One such fiber is Antron or trilobal nylon (a yarn used in carpeting). It is shiny, translucent, and comes in a variety of colors. Another example of useful artificial fibers is bristles from an artist's paint brush. These make very durable tails for mayfly duns and spinners but are especially good when constructing caddis emergers and adults. Such fibers are great for the antennae of these and other insects. The structure of an emergent caddis is a very noticeable characteristic and should also be incorporated in the artificial.

Where very shiny bodies are required, some of the synthetics will fit the bill because they are usually more reflective than natural fur. But there are some natural fibers that have been overlooked for years and can be very useful in pattern development. Duck rump has many intriguing possibilities, some of which we have suggested; almost certainly many more uses will be discovered in the future. Another natural, pheasant rump, is now being used by classic-salmon-fly tyers. This is a near perfect substitute for the blue heron used on Spey-type salmon flies. It is also a great material for the legs on mayfly nymphs and caddisfly pupae, wing cases for nymphs and emergers, and tails on nymphs.

It is not enough to have a thorough knowledge of the methods of emergence and an acceptable artificial that can be fished to simulate the action of the naturals. The fly fisherman must be able to cast and manipulate the fly correctly, and this is not easily accomplished. The first and second requirements are intellectual in nature, and most fly fishermen are intellectual or they would not be fly fishermen in the first place. The third requirement, casting, requires some physical coordination and considerable practice—of a very specific sort. Fly casting is somewhat like skiing. Each skill requires five or six muscular movements that must be performed in an exact sequence. If one motion is overpowered or underpowered or made a little too early or too late, the whole process of casting, or turning when skiing, falls apart.

Fly casting, like skiing, also requires practice. Furthermore, manipulating the artificial once it is cast correctly, requires even more practice. An excellent place to work on this physical skill is a good-sized backyard lawn. Manipulation skills can also be worked on while fishing when no action is taking place. (For further information on casting and manipulating techniques see *Fly Fishing Strategy*.)

We hope the last two chapters of this work give the angler some new ideas and methods to work with. If all three skills are learned (action of immatures at hatch time, correct fly-pattern selection, and skillful casting and fly manipulation) the angler will have a much more pleasant and productive experience on the stream. It is our hope the contents of this book will allow all fly fishers many action-filled days on the river, with more landed and released trout—especially when there is an interesting aquatic-insect emergence.

Selected Bibliography

ARBONA, FRED L., JR. *Mayflies, the Angler, and the Trout.* Lyons & Burford, 1989.

BAUMAN, RICHARD W. AND ARDEN R., AND REBECCA F. SURDICK. *Stoneflies of the Rocky Mountains.* American Entomological Society at the Academy of Natural Sciences, 1977.

BETTS, JOHN. *Synthetic Flies.* Privately printed, 1980.

CLARKE, BRIAN, AND JOHN GODDARD. *The Trout and the Fly.* Lyons & Burford, 1980.

EDMONDS, GEORGE F. JR. *Mayflies of Utah (Ephemeroptera).* University of Massachusetts (thesis), 1952.

————. *Biogeography and Evolution of Ephemeroptera.* Annals of Revisional Entomology, 17:21–43, 1972.

EDMUNDS, GEORGE F., JR., STEVEN L. JENSON, AND LEWIS BERNER. *The Mayflies of Northern Central America.* University of Minnesota Press, 1976.

EDMUNDS, GEORGE F., JR., AND W. P. McCAFFERTY. *The Mayfly Subimago. Purdue Experiment Station Journal,* No. 11, 150. Annual Reviews, Entomology, 33:509–29, 1988.

HARRIS, J. R. *An Angler's Entomology,* 1952.

HUTCHINGS, ROSS E. *The World of Dragon Flies and Damsel Flies.* Dodd, Mead, 1969.

JENSEN, S. L. *The Mayflies of Idaho.* University of Utah (unpublished thesis).

LaFONTAINE, GARY. *Caddisflies.* Lyons & Burford, 1981.

LEONARD, J. W., AND F. A. LEONARD. *Mayflies of Michigan Trout Streams.* Cranbrook Institute, 1962.

————. *An Annotated List of Michigan Trichoptera. Occasional Papers of the Museum of Zoology,* University of Michigan Press, Number 522, 1949.

116

———. *Noteworthy Records of Caddis Flies from Michigan with Descriptions of New Species. Occasional Papers of the Museum of Zoology,* University of Michigan Press, Number 520, 1949.

McCAFFERTY, W. PATRICK. *Aquatic Entomology for the Fly Fisherman.* Jones & Bartlett, 1981.

MERRITT, R. W., AND K. W. CUMMINS. *An Introduction to the Aquatic Insects of North America.* Kendall Hunt Publishing Company, 1978.

NEEDHAM, J. G., J. R. TRAVEG, AND Y. HSU. *The Biology of Mayflies.* Comstock Publishing, 1935.

ROSS, HERBERT H. *The Caddis Flies or Trichoptera of Illinois.* State of Illinois, 1944.

SCHWIEBERT, ERNEST G. *Nymphs.* Winchester Press, 1973.

WATERS, T. F. *Invertebrate Drift—Ecology and Significance to Stream Fishes.* Symposium on Salmon and Trout in Streams, 121–134. Institute of Fisheries, the University of British Columbia. Paper number 6452, Scientific Journal series, Minnesota Agricultural Experiment Station, 1968.

WATSON, CHARLES. *Black Fly Emergence.* Clemson University, ND.

WHITLOCK, DAVE. *Dave Whitlock's Guide to Aquatic Trout Foods.* Lyons & Burford, 1982.

WRIGHT, LEONARD M., JR. "The Case of the Delicious, Mysterious Caddis," *Sports Afield,* May 1979.

Index